# CAIN, Come Home!

# CAIN, Come Home!

by

Paul G. Bretscher

Clayton Publishing House
St. Louis, Missouri

CAIN, Come Home!

Paul G. Bretscher

Original Art Concepts by
Joel Paul Bretscher



CLAYTON PUBLISHING HOUSE
P. O. Box 9258
St. Louis, Missouri 63117





Library of Congress No. 76-1810
ISBN 0-915644-05-3

To Amalia Erickson Melcher, Marguerite's Mother
And to Our Sisters and Brothers

Amalia (Pecky) Hess
Dorothea E. Wessler †
Ruth Ressmeyer
Esther Gruell
Carl W. Bretscher
Manuel M. Bretscher

# CONTENTS

# PREFACE

*You Can't Go Home Again,* wrote Thomas Wolfe. Too many things change in life. We have no way of reconstructing what is past.

Following man's departure from Eden, that seemed to be his inevitable fate. There was one ray of hope in a divine promise given. But when Cain murdered his brother Abel, the barriers between man and God appeared to be insurmountable.

Now here is Paul Bretscher inviting Cain and his descendants to come home. In doing so he expresses the major themes of scripture with freshness and provocative insight that reflect years of scholarly study and teaching, as well as substantial experience as a parish pastor. He discusses the familiar topics of man's wickedness and God's grace. But he does so in a most unusual manner.

First, Dr. Bretscher chooses an interesting central character and a different way of looking at the motivations which lead him on. The story about Cain is really the story about us all. The "knowledge of good and evil" which weighs heavily on mankind includes the seeking of pleasure and the avoiding of pain. While that knowledge can be constructive, within limits, it is also destructive in its consequences. "The problem called 'sin,'" Dr. Bretscher points out, "arises only when we seize upon this capacity of ours and absolutize it as though it were our *only* reality as human beings. . . . We are still creatures, under God. The 'beginning of wisdom' lies not in our eyesight, but in 'the fear of the Lord.'"

A second intriguing development in Dr. Bretscher's account deals with the problem of alienation in Cain and the rest of mankind. This process makes the self the center of reference, as each person calculates his own advantage. The result is fearfulness, separation from God, and antagonism toward other people.

The alienated are those who occupy what Dr. Bretscher calls Enochville, the city named after Cain's son, but which is the secular society where we all live. This society might be sophisticated and culturally advanced. Living by the knowledge of good and evil can be socially workable, Dr. Bretscher says, but "justice in Enochville is a form of accommodation to alienation." Since such a society depends upon the discipline of law and order, the Hobbesian idea of government gets some support.

While there are certain forms of love in the secular society, they do not really transcend personal advantage. The alienated society does not know how to become the reconciled society. This leads Dr. Bretscher to the third emphasis of his book, the process of reconciliation through Christ. The shedding of blood becomes significant again, this time not Abel's blood crying out for vengeance, but Jesus' blood calling for mercy and forgiveness.

Now Cain and all the rest of us can come home again. Our relationship with God has changed. So has our relationship with ourselves, with other people, and with the earth that gives us sustenance. We no longer carry the mark of Cain upon ourselves but the mark of our Lord Jesus Christ.

As a theologian, Dr. Bretscher delves deeply into the Scriptures, even explicating some of his findings in the appendix of the book. As a working pastor, however, he is more concerned about the way in which God's people live out the newness of their lives. He warns: "The weapons of Satan's testing are many, and no child of God escapes the battle . . . The enemy is sin couching at the door. . . ." He therefore calls for the humility of a "barefoot church" and a "barefoot listening" to the Word of God.

We have things to do in Enochville. Our task, says Dr. Bretscher, is to live in our society with all its temptations and troubles, being useful citizens, and seeking to capture the hearts of its inhabitants with our secret weapon—the only one we have—the Spirit of Christ.

Dr. Bretscher writes thoughtfully and well. Perhaps his finest contribution is to provide us with a new perspective on a familiar landscape. Reading it is like standing at the top of a hill on a clear day. We look back down the long road into the past and see the twists and turns of history. We visualize the endless hosts of men and women who have passed along the way, with all their faults, their ingenuity, and their capacity. And then we look ahead to where the road will lead us. We know that walking with our God we shall have opportunities for living lives of rich fulfillment. In the dim distance we catch a glimpse of a great city—not the tawdry Enochville of our contemporary world but the golden gleam of the Eternal City of our God.

"Cain, Come Home!" As we resume our journey, we can hear the voice of invitation—if we will.

A. G. Huegli

# ACKNOWLEDGMENTS

This book originated in the summer and fall of 1970 as an essay on alienation and reconciliation, which I was privileged to present to the presidents and other leaders of The Lutheran Church—Missouri Synod and its districts at eight regional conferences in the United States and Canada. I was invited thereafter to share the material also at a number of pastoral conferences in various districts. The Texas District, under President Carl A. Heckmann and executives Ray C. Schkade, Keith Loomans, and Eugene F. Gruell, even arranged for the lecture to be recorded on tape, so that it might be used as a resource for a district-wide program of "Gospel Revitalization."

It was a unique joy to me to present *Cain, Come Home!* also to about 400 ladies of the Lutheran Women's Missionary League, who gathered for a retreat at Beverly Shores, Indiana in May 1972. Sponsored by the Kankakee Valley Zone under the presidency of Mrs. Karl (Norma) Wurster, the retreat numbered among its guests the officers of the Indiana District LWML, including its President, Mrs. Ross Jennings.

In its present form the book has benefited considerably from my personal growth during these five intervening years. My interest in submitting it for publication was revived chiefly by my brother Carl, pastor of Immanuel Lutheran Church, Las Vegas, New Mexico. After our father, Paul M. Bretscher, had died on August 10, 1974, Carl found a copy of the manuscript on his desk and read it. I am grateful to Carl for his enthusiasm, as well as to Manuel and others in our family, to whom this book is dedicated.

I continue to be grateful to the synodical and district presidents and other leaders, most of them still in offices, who participated with me in the regional conferences. A special word of thanks is due to President Albert G. Huegli of Valparaiso University, not only for contributing the Preface, but also for perceptive insights that have helped the manuscript. My wife remembers him as a beloved teacher years ago when she attended St. John's College, Winfield, Kansas. He and his wife Rae have become very dear to us during our years at Valparaiso University and at Immanuel Lutheran Church.

Let me express my appreciation also to Laura Prahl, Dorothy Czamanske, and Mary Gussick Lohrbach for typing the manuscript in earlier stages; to my congregation, Immanuel, for trusting me so generously with freedom to share in giving and receiving with the church beyond our parish; and to Marguerite and our children for their love and patience.

Apparently the time has come for *Cain, Come Home!* to appear as a book. May our Lord use it as he will!

PAUL G. BRETSCHER
Advent, 1975

# INTRODUCTION

Years ago in prep school I learned two quotations from the Greek philosopher Archimedes. One was "Eureka" (I found it!)—supposedly uttered when he noticed how the water rose as he sat down in the bath tub, and thus discovered the principle of displacement and flotation.

The other, which concerns me here, was the excited boast, "Give me a place to stand, and I shall move the earth!"—spoken when Archimedes had understood mathematically how a man could amplify his strength indefinitely by the use of levers. The boast was hyperbole, of course. Archimedes had no literal intention of moving the earth. He was only projecting large, in fanciful exaggeration, his vision of the enormous possibilities of engineering and technology.

Two things about that sentence intrigue me, however. First, Archimedes concedes that he must have *a place to stand.* Technical and mathematical brains, the equipment of fulcrum and lever, the exertion of force—all these are meaningless unless he has good, reliable ground under his feet. Secondly, the philosopher concedes that such ground is not something he can supply. It must be *given* him.

Archimedes' little text is a parable. Men have always had visions, but the capacity to turn a vision into reality requires a place to stand. We tell a dreamer to "come down to earth," for he can accomplish nothing unless he "keeps his feet on the ground." The batter in baseball sets his feet with great care. He knows the importance of a firm "place to stand." The political realist likewise pays close attention to his ground. He knows what resources are available to be harnessed, and what limitations must be respected. If he loses contact with his "place to stand," all his energy and rhetoric will accomplish nothing.

The church has been given a place to stand, not the "sand" of our natural impulses and wisdom, but solid "rock." If anyone builds his house, that is, his life upon this "rock," Jesus promises that all the winds and floods he experiences will not be able to shatter or overthrow him (Matthew 7:24-27). The apostles knew this rock and how to stand upon it. The rock was God's unfailing word and promise, spoken to them out of the history of Jesus Christ, crucified and risen again. From that rock they moved the earth. As Acts 17:7 has it, they "turned the world upside down." They inverted human perceptions and values, set people truly free, made them a new creation. I shall describe the transformation in terms of the biblical themes of *alienation* and *reconciliation*. The earth to be moved was humanity in its alienation. The goal of the moving was the reconciliation of people with God and with one another. The goal was accomplished by setting them "high upon a rock" (Psalm 27:5; 61:2).

The task of this book is to explore the "rock" and what it means to stand upon it. It is necessary to begin, however, with the alternative of "sand," that is, with the problem of alienation. For this my basic text is the narrative of Cain in Genesis 4. The story tells how the alienation began, and belongs to the Bible's way of describing what alienation is.

# PART ONE

# CAIN

## The Story of Alienation

# *Cain: The Story of Alienation*

**Genesis 4**

*Now Adam knew Eve his wife, and she conceived and bore Cain, saying, "I have gotten a man with the help of the LORD." And again, she bore his brother Abel. Now Abel was a keeper of sheep, and Cain a tiller of the ground.*

*In the course of time Cain brought to the LORD an offering of the fruit of the ground, and Abel brought of the firstlings of his flock and of their fat portions. And the LORD had regard for Abel and his offering, but for Cain and his offering he had no regard. So Cain was very angry, and his countenance fell. The LORD said to Cain, "Why are you angry, and why has your countenance fallen? If you do well, will you not be accepted? And if you do not do well, sin is couching at the door; its desire is for you, but you must master it."*

*Cain said to Abel his brother, "Let us go out to the field." And when they were in the field, Cain rose up against his brother Abel, and killed him.*

*Then the LORD said to Cain, "Where is Abel your brother?"*

*He said, "I do not know; am I my brother's keeper?"*

*And the LORD said, "What have you done? The voice of your brother's blood is crying to me from the ground. And now you are cursed from the ground, which has opened its mouth to receive your brother's blood from your hand. When you till the ground, it shall no longer yield to you its strength; you shall be a fugitive and a wanderer on the earth."*

*Cain said to the LORD, "My punishment is greater than I can bear. Behold, thou hast driven me this day away from the ground; and from thy face I shall be hidden; and I shall be a fugitive and a wanderer on the earth, and whoever finds me will slay me."*

*Then the LORD said to him, "Not so! If any one slays Cain, vengeance shall be taken on him sevenfold." And the LORD put a mark on Cain, lest any who came upon him should kill him. Then Cain went away from the presence of the LORD, and dwelt in the land of Nod, east of Eden.*

*Cain knew his wife, and she conceived and bore Enoch; and he built a city, and called the name of the city after the name of his son, Enoch. To Enoch was born Irad; and Irad was the father of Mehujael, and Mehujael the father of Methushael and Methushael the father of Lamech.*

*And Lamech took two wives; the name of the one was Adah, and the name of the other was Zillah. Adah bore Jabal; he was the father of those who dwell in tents and have cattle. His brother's name was Jubal; he was the father of all those who play the lyre and pipe. Zillah bore Tubal-cain; he was the forger of all instruments of bronze and iron. The sister of Tubal-cain was Naamah.*

*Lamech said to his wives:*

*"Adah and Zillah, hear my voice;*
*you wives of Lamech, hearken to what I say:*
*I have slain a man for wounding me,*
*a young man for striking me.*
*If Cain is avenged sevenfold,*
*truly Lamech seventy-sevenfold."*

*And Adam knew his wife again, and she bore a son and called his name Seth, for she said, "God has appointed for me another child instead of Abel, for Cain slew him." To Seth also a son was born, and he called his name Enosh. At that time men began to call upon the name of the LORD.*

**Genesis 6: 1-8**

*When men began to multiply on the face of the ground, and daughters were born to them, the sons of God saw that the daughters of men were fair; and they took to wife such of them as they chose. Then the LORD said, "My spirit shall not abide in man for ever, for he is flesh, but his days shall be a hundred and twenty years." The Nephilim were on the earth in those days, and also afterward, when the sons of God came in to the daughters of men, and they bore children to them. These were the mighty men that were of old, the men of renown.*

*The LORD saw that the wickedness of man was great in the earth, and that every imagination of the thoughts of his heart was only evil con-*

*tinually. And the LORD was sorry that he had made man on the earth, and it grieved him to his heart. So the LORD said, "I will blot out man whom I have created from the face of the ground, man and beast and creeping things and birds of the air, for I am sorry that I have made them." But Noah found favor in the eyes of the LORD.*

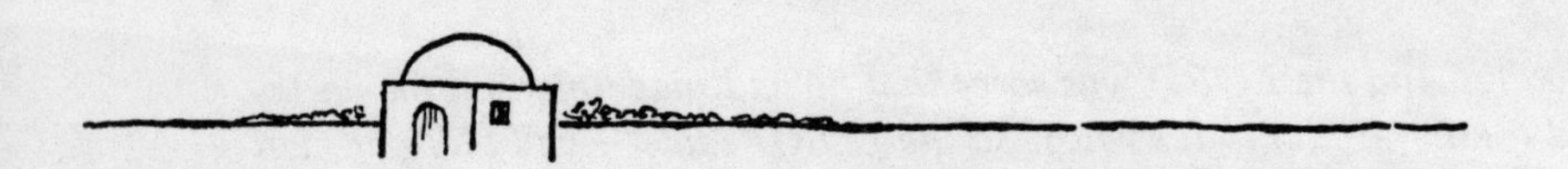

## Chapter 1

# *THE AMBUSH*

*"Sin is couching at the door; its desire is for you, but you must master it."* Genesis 4: 7

The root cause of Cain's alienation is called "sin." It is personified as a predatory animal, hungry to pounce upon Cain the moment he goes out the door.

### The Meaning of "Sin"

We must pause to consider what this "sin" is, which lies in ambush for Cain. The story of the fall in Genesis 2 and 3 portrays it as a violation of God's clear command, "Of the tree of *the knowledge of good and evil* you shall not eat, for in the day you eat of it, you shall die" (Gen. 2:17).

"Good and evil" are not moral terms here, as when we speak of good and bad behavior. Good stands rather for what attracts us as desirable, and evil for what repels us. Already at a very early age a child experiences the force of such attraction and repulsion. He "knows how to refuse the evil and choose the good," as Isaiah 7:15 puts it. In a graphic parable Jesus portrays the difference between a rich man who in his lifetime received "*good* things," and a poor man, Lazarus, who received "*evil* things" (Luke 16:25). Whenever we notice such glaring disparities as this, we experience a characteristic reaction. We would gladly participate in the "good," but not in the "evil." We would like to be the rich man, but would avoid being a Lazarus.

Such an impulse in itself is not yet what the biblical diagnosis means by "sin." God himself offers the trees of his garden to us as "pleasant to the sight and good for food" (Genesis 2:9). Their attractiveness, together with our capacity to see and be attracted, belongs to the wonder of God's grace to us. Indeed, when the Lord expressly says, "You may freely eat of every tree" (Genesis 2:17), he even honors the variety of our tastes. He does not object if someone prefers apples to avocados.

Furthermore, it is by virtue of God's own image (Genesis 1:25-27) or breath (Genesis 2:7) in us that we enjoy and exercise creative dominion over the world into which he has placed us. The challenge to "till and keep" the garden (Genesis 2:15) implies that we, by exercising our wisdom and common sense, shall work toward achieving what we see to be good and advantageous for us, and toward avoiding what threatens evil. Our capacity for curiosity and discovery, for imagination and inventiveness, for learning and transmission of learning, is the very instrument of our desire to enjoy, enlarge, and preserve good over against evil. In this wholesome and positive sense our "knowledge of good and evil" corresponds to God's own. By it we concur in God's judgment that his creation is "very good" (Genesis 1:31). By it a man and a woman see beauty in one another, and accept the unity of marriage as a great good (Genesis 2:23-25). By it we understand what the commandment means to "love your neighbor as yourself" (Leviticus 19:18), namely, to seek the good of our neighbor and to overcome what is hurting him, just as we do for ourselves.

Thus the difference between pleasure and pain as we experience these is in no way to be obscured. If we know God, we praise him for our enjoyments as the God who wants us to have such joy. We also cry to him in our sufferings as the God who knows our griefs, bears them with us, and wants to deliver us from evil. Similarly, if we know God in our neighbor, we understand what it means to "rejoice with those who rejoice and weep with those who weep" (Romans 12:15).

It belongs to our very humanness, therefore, that we constantly notice and act on the difference between good and evil. The problem called "sin" arises only when we seize upon this capacity of ours and absolutize it as though it were our *only* reality as human beings. We forget, then, that to be human and wise and creative does not make us "like God" in our "knowing good and evil" (Genesis 3:5). We are still creatures, under God. The "beginning of wisdom" lies not in our eyesight, but in "the fear of the Lord" (Psalm 111:10). We are not God. We do not know good and evil in any ultimate sense. We cannot see the future or anticipate all consequences. If we imagine that, by applying our knowledge of good and evil, we can create life for ourselves or establish our worth, we are utter fools. The glory of any person on God's earth is not to be measured by the heights to which he climbs over other people, as he engineers for himself a maximum of "good" and a minimum of "evil." Our glory is rather to know the Lord who delights to be gracious to us. And our wisdom begins when we hold our knowledge of good and evil loosely, so as to entrust the ultimate of such knowledge to him.

This is the thrust of the story of the fall in Genesis 3. An alternative voice enters, the voice of a slithering serpent. It finds the woman alone, and encourages her to think and act in isolation, without reference to God or neighbor. What matters is simply what she can see with her own eyes. If she is to be fully a person, she must assert herself by making up her own mind, in terms of the advantages to be gained. Can she *see* God or the death against which God has warned her? What she cannot *see,* she must not fear! Can she *see* how desirable the fruit is, "good for food" and a "delight to the eyes"? Can she *see* how important it is to assert her own wisdom and thus be independent and free? If so, she must take and eat! Thus the limitations of humanness are shattered. From now on life consists in getting what one wants and avoiding what one does not want. Wanting and not wanting become supreme. The biblical diagnosis acknowledges that the woman has become "wise," but with a wisdom that is death to her and to the whole humanity which eats this fruit with her. "The knowledge of good and evil" has risen up against and displaced the knowledge of the Lord.

The startling biblical commandment, "You shall not covet" (Exodus 20:17; Romans 7:7), exposes this root sin. In 1 John 2:16

it is amplified as "the lust of the flesh and the lust of the eyes and the pride of life." James 1:14-15 unfolds its progression: "Each person is tempted when he is lured and enticed by his own desire. Then desire when it has conceived gives birth to sin; and sin when it is full-grown brings forth death."

The obverse of covetousness is *fear* of what threatens "evil." In the story of the fall *fear* is sin's most immediate consequence. The man and the woman hide from God. Hoping to make themselves presentable, they invent clothing of fig leaves. Perhaps they can distract attention from their guilt, and even win a compliment! They squirm to escape blame by shifting it elsewhere. This is the way of the serpent. Humankind slithers in the dirt, darting back and forth to seize every proximate good and to avoid every threatening evil, discovering and crawling through the smallest loophole. It is an appropriate posture, the biblical witness declares, for "dirt is what you are, and to dirt you shall return."

### The "Sin" that Couches for Cain

The narrative of Cain builds on the contrast between knowing the Lord and knowing good and evil. As the story begins, Cain knows the Lord and the Lord knows him. Cain's very name implies that his life and identity is rooted in Yahweh. "I have gotten a man with the help of the Lord," Eve says. The relationship between Cain and God is quite positive. The fact that Yahweh enters freely into conversation with Cain at the point of Cain's anger suggests that they have been on speaking terms all along. As for Cain's offering, we are told explicitly that he brought it "to the Lord."

We need to be wary, therefore, of the traditional supposition that Cain is already being thought of as a sinner in connection with his sacrifice. The story as written does not suggest that Cain's offering was somehow defective. No cause is specified as to why Yahweh should have had "no regard for Cain and his offering." This has always been a stumbling-block, however. Somehow we take this sentence to imply that Yahweh is expressing his disapproval, and we want to know why. One commentator will make the point that Yahweh preferred a pastoral culture to an agrarian. Another will speculate that Cain brought the Lord merely "fruits," whereas Abel brought "firstlings" and "fat" portions. A New Testament text like Hebrews 11:4 is cited for its accent on Abel's "faith," the ready inference being that Cain was lacking in "faith" or "sincerity." Similarly, 1 John 3:11-12 explains that Cain murdered his brother "because his own deeds were evil and his brother's righteous." This last, as we shall see in chapter 4, is not so much a commentary on our text, however, as on the hatred Jesus experienced from those who "loved darkness rather than light, because *their deeds were evil.*" (John 3:19)

I shall deal further with these New Testament passages in an appendix, for their testimony needs to be heard and understood. Our immediate task, though, is to take our text seriously as it stands. Out of such seriousness we discover that the holy writer *is not even concerned* with our question of cause!

The very point of our text, and the force of Cain's temptation, is that *there is no particular cause at all why the Lord should pay no attention to Cain and his offering, or why God should take such note of Abel!* The significance of the contrast between Yahweh's "looking upon" the one and "not looking" upon the other is simply that God acts in the counsel of his own freedom, and distributes his gifts according to his own wisdom and will.

The verb here translated "have regard for" is quite rare. Its literal and root meaning seems to be "look." Yet similar constructions, with other Hebrew verbs to express God's "looking" upon people, are not uncommon. In 1 Samuel 1, for example, we are told how the Lord blesses Peninnah with children, but closes the womb of Hannah. Why does Yahweh treat the two wives of Elkanah so unequally? No answer is given to that question. Hannah prays Yahweh to "look upon" her affliction, to "remember" and "not forget" her (verse 11), and the Lord answers by "remembering" her and giving her a son (verse 19). Apparently God's "looking" upon someone implies the bestowal of blessings, while his "not looking" implies the withholding of blessings. Similarly when Elizabeth, so long barren, had conceived the son to be named John, she hid herself for five months saying, "Thus the Lord has done to me in the days when he *looked on me*" (Luke 1:25). The implication is that in her barrenness the Lord had not been looking on her. Yet we do not and must not interpret this "looking" or "not looking" to imply a divine judgment on some attitude or action God saw in her. No such inference is allowable.

We trust God to know what he is doing when he gives gifts or withholds them according to his wisdom and pleasure. In the story of Cain and Abel, the point of Yahweh's looking on the one brother and his sacrifice and not on the other, is that the Lord, contrary to our natural notion of fairness and rights, proceeds to treat the brothers unequally. *Why* does God bless the one, and withhold blessings from or even lay special burdens upon the other? We cannot know his intentions. We can only entrust "the knowledge of good and evil" to the Lord, rely on his wisdom and promises, and wait it out in the confidence that ultimately God is not intending to hurt either a Hannah or a Cain, just as he is not really conferring unjust advantages on a Peninnah or an Abel.

Now, however, we are ready to appreciate the force of Cain's temptation. As people who ourselves "know good and evil" when we see it, we protest against such unequal treatment. But God dismisses our protest. "Am I not allowed to do what I choose with what belongs to me? Is your eye evil because I am good?" he asks the vineyard worker (Matthew 20:15). Moses has to learn this. What is the strange "goodness" of God which inheres in the very name Yahweh? The Lord answers, "I will be gracious to whom I will be gracious, and will show mercy on whom I will show mercy" (Exodus 33:18-19). Job surrenders to that kind of "goodness" when he asks, "Shall we receive good at the hand of God, and shall we not receive evil?" (Job 2:10).

St. Paul confronts the question boldly in Romans 9. Why should God speak the promise to Isaac and not to Ishmael? Why does he tell Rebecca, "The elder shall serve the younger," and punctuate it even more dramatically in Malachi 1:2-3, "Jacob I loved, but Esau I hated."? Why should Yahweh take Israel to be his people, and harden Pharaoh and the Gentile world as outsiders from his promises? Our whole natural instinct, our "knowledge of good and evil" sentiment, rises in protest against such "injustice on God's part" (Romans 9:14). But it is our instinct that errs, not God! St. Paul quotes the definition of God's "goodness" from Exodus 33:19. He adds a little commentary of his own, "So it depends not upon man's will or exertion, but upon God's mercy" (Romans 9:16). He pleads that the clay trust the potter. When God's wisdom and purpose has unfolded to the end, then we shall know how to praise "the depth of the riches and wisdom and knowledge of God" (Romans 11:33-36).

What hits Cain so hard is his experience of "injustice on God's part" (Romans 9:14). Somehow the fact that the Lord took note of Abel and his offering, but paid no attention to Cain, must have become clearly evident, visible to the eye. In my old Sunday School lessons the evidence was depicted artistically in the movement of smoke, Abel's going upward and Cain's downward. Much more likely the writer had in mind a series of benefits which Abel experienced, whereas Cain suffered a series of reverses, one trouble or disappointment or frustration after another. Abel's flocks were fruitful. Cain's field yielded thorns and thistles. The text makes it perfectly clear, however, that both the prosperity and the adversity, both the "good" and the "evil," come from one and the same God. There is not a hint of polytheism, as though a shepherd deity were opposed to an agrarian, a kind god to a spiteful one. There is only one Yahweh, who "has regard for" the one brother and not for the other.

Thus Cain is tempted. His eyes are open to the good and to the evil. Will he live by that eyesight? Or will he trust himself to the word and will of the Lord his God even *against* what he sees? Can he trust the Potter to do what he will with the clay? Can he take the lower place, and see his brother in the higher, without resentment, without fearing that God is thereby rejecting him, or making him inferior, or punishing him for something?

The problem for us is as real as ever. We always want to infer from God's treatment of us what his thoughts are toward us. That is why we, like Cain, are readily overpowered by our sense of injustice when we feel we are not getting our fair share. Joseph's brothers resented what appeared to be favoritism on their father's part toward Joseph (Genesis 37:4). This resentment was the root of their sin, and it nearly ended, like Cain's, in murder.

I struggle with this frequently in my own family of ten, for the children have a startling capacity to detect what they see as injustice. It is no easy matter for me as a father to be "gracious to whom I choose to be gracious." Nathan, our second youngest, needed a bicycle. Already last summer he had outgrown the little twenty-inch bike he was riding, and I had promised to do something about it this year. The rest of the children had bicycles. So I brought the matter up at table a couple of times. Were they willing for me to invest forty dollars in a bike for Nathan who needed it, without holding out their own hands for forty dollars and thus jacking up the price to $400? They were not willing. Some of them had invested their own money in bicycles, and Nathan, though he had no money, should pay for his. Finally one day I stopped with the four youngest boys at the bike store. The owner had a good-looking used bike for thirty dollars. Would the other three let me buy that bike for Nathan? "Yes," said little Matthew, still too young to "refuse the evil and choose the good," as Isaiah 7:15 has it. "No," said Joel and Seth in their wise determination to refuse so great an evil. I laughed at them and bought the bicycle anyway. That evening I noticed that Joel, every time he got near Nathan, was muttering at him under his breath, "Joseph! Joseph!"

Abel, of course, is tempted too. How will he receive the exceptional blessings God is heaping on him? Will he accept them humbly and in a spirit of thanksgiving, as coming to him by God's mercy alone? Could he just as freely let it all go? Or will he see these good gifts as evidences of some special favor, as proof that he is somehow superior to Cain and more righteous than he? Will Abel love and support and comfort Cain, and even weep with him without lording it over him or being condescending to him? Abel's temptation is more subtle than Cain's. We succumb to that one without even realizing what has happened to us, or how alienated we have become from God even while imagining we are close to him and basking in his favor!

### Cain's Fall

Our story, however, concentrates on the tragedy of Cain. Cain's reaction is very human and accords altogether with "the knowledge of good and evil." "Cain was very angry," we are told, "and his countenance fell." His eyes are wide open. He is not blind or stupid. With every new blessing Abel enjoys, and with every new adversity that befalls Cain, the anger grows. It is not fair! Cain works as hard as Abel does, perhaps even harder. Besides, he is the older, the first-born. Behind all the anger is Cain's protest against God. What good is it to sacrifice and to pray if God treats him like that?

Cain's thoughts churn within him, building up pressure to the point of explosion. Is there anything Abel can say to him or do for him which would not be interpreted as an insult? What can people today, who have all the visible advantages, say to those who feel oppressed, unjustly treated, discriminated against, filled with the indignation that belongs to self-pity, ready to let their jealous anger explode in hatred and reprisal? In his fallen face and angry heart Cain already reflects alienation. The text, however, does not yet regard him as having fallen. He has only felt the force of temptation. The battle is on.

Yahweh himself intervenes, for Cain must see reality in a different way. God has not cast Cain off. "Why are you angry, and why has your countenance fallen?" The next question, literally translated, would read, "Is there not, if you did good, a lifting?" I take the "lifting" to refer still to Cain's facial expression, as in the Aaronic blessing, "The Lord lift up his countenance upon you" (Numbers 6:26; Psalm 4:6). A smiling face would signal trust and good will, a fallen face portends disaster. We might paraphrase, "If your attitude were good, wouldn't you be smiling? But if it is not good, sin is couching at the door." Cain's real enemy is not God, and not Abel, but *sin*. Not the disadvantage he is experiencing, but his response to that disadvantage, is the deadly beast now couching to destoy him, which Cain must see and master! Yahweh pleads for Cain to surrender his own knowledge of good and evil, to cling to God even in adversity, and to stand in hope and trust on the sure ground of God's word and promise.

Cain, however, gives no sign that he has heard even one word of what God is saying to him. We can well understand his torment and anger. The Word of God is just words! Abel gets concrete advantages, all Cain gets is words! The visible reality is the only truth that interests Cain—the reality of prosperous Abel, so superior, God's favorite! To cut Abel down to size is all Cain can think of now. The ambush is ripe; Cain speaks to Abel. Ancient translations report that he said, "Let us go out to the field." Is that all that was said? It doesn't really matter.

What matters now is only the act, the climactic violence of brother against brother, when the wisdom of knowing good and evil reaches fruition and "sin" pounces. Cain kills. The killing is of a piece with all the stress and bitterness that has led up to it—just as the woman's eating the fruit was of a piece with her looking at it, admiring it, wanting it. The act, however, is decisive. All that preceded has belonged to the process of temptation, but once the act is complete, it all belongs to the sin. Heart and act have now merged in a union which every human hatred approves (1 John 3:15). It is done. There is no turning back. Abel is dead. In another but equally real sense, so is Cain.

The depth of Cain's alienation is now exposed step by step. Here, as in Genesis 3, the Lord intervenes to reopen conversation with the sinner. That he does so is a great "good," yet Cain, like Adam and Eve, much prefers to be left alone. The question, "Where is Abel, your brother?" begets a lie and a shrug, "I do not know. Am I my brother's keeper?" The God who was not deceived by fig leaves sees through Cain, too. If Abel's tongue is silent, his blood is not. It cries to Yahweh from the ground, indicating the murderer.

Thus Cain has not achieved the "good" he sought, and which "sin" promised him. No longer can he in righteous indignation accuse God and Abel of injustice. He is now the accused! Even the blood-soaked ground curses him, and refuses to serve him or yield its fruit to him. Cain has no defense. He ought, then, to collapse in tears, confess the whole horror, and throw himself on God's mercy. But he does not. He retreats rather into self-pity, the last defense of the alienated, "My punishment is greater than I can bear," and into the self-conscious dread that suspects every man as enemy, "Whoever finds me will slay me."

Yet alienated man does adjust to living "without God in the world," as Ephesians 2:12 puts it. God will have it so. He puts a mark of sevenfold vengeance on Cain, a threat to anyone who would kill him. If people cannot love and honor one another in the face of their apparent inequalities, then let them live in fear of one another! Perhaps the threat of vengeance, the dread of death, will restrain the momentum of hatred and murder, brother against brother! Cain goes out from the presence (literally "face") of Yahweh to the land called Nod (Wandering), east of Eden. His back is turned to the Lord.

**The Society of Cain**

The adjustment of alienated man to life in alienation is detailed in the account of the society that descends from Cain. The city named "Enoch," after Cain's son, signifies civilization, government, people allied under a common cause of desire and fear, self-interest and defense. Cain's society is inventive. Jabal's tent provides a portable home for wandering nomads in their care of cattle. Jubal's lyre and pipe embellish civilization with music, art, and story-telling. Tubalcain's metallurgy in bronze and iron points to technological progress in tools and weaponry. Lamech, alienated from God and therefore needing his wives as the audience for his self-justification, sings, "I have slain a man for wounding me, a young man for striking me. If Cain is avenged sevenfold, truly Lamech seventy-sevenfold." It was self-defense, after all. Thus Lamech affirms the principles of justice and law enforcement, so essential to the society of Cain. Vengeance, threat, fear, power—these are instruments of order, the best answer alienated man can give toward preserving at least a tensioned peace in a world consumed by desire and fear.

The last paragraph of Genesis 4 tells of the family of Seth, and how men began to "call on the name of Yahweh." Two very different societies exist in the world now, one consisting of those who know the Lord, the other of those who live apart from God by their knowledge of good and evil. As these societies multiply, they come into contact with each other again. The result is portrayed in Genesis 6. Seth's society fails to reconcile Cain's to God. On the contrary, Cain's corrupts Seth's, absorbing it into the fascinations of its own alienation. That, I am persuaded, is what the holy writer had in mind, regardless of what the contrasting terminology "sons of God" and "daughters of men" may have meant in ancient pagan mythologies.

> *When men began to multiply on the face of the ground, and daughters were born to them, the sons of God saw that the daughters of men were fair; and they took to wife such of them as they chose.* (Genesis 6:1-2)

The children of Israel, whose literature this was, would readily understand "sons of God" to mean those who "call upon the name of Yahweh" (Genesis 4:20; Psalm 116:13, 17; Joel 2:32; 1 Corinthians 1:2), for Yahweh had conferred the name "my son" on Israel in the history of the Exodus (Exodus 4:22-23). The descendants of Seth are related to God in a way that corresponds to Israel's own sonship. "Sons of God" is non-sexual terminology here, standing for God's people. "Daughters of men" is the contrasting term, applied now to the alienated race of Cain, but suggesting also the seductivity of Cain's civilization. The passage implies not merely literal intermarriage, politically expedient and necessary as this may have been, but cultural alliance and intercourse between the two societies.

As the holy writer describes it, however, the force behind such intermarriage is simply "the knowledge of good and evil." "The sons of God *saw* that the daughters of men were *fair* ("good," as in Genesis 3:5, 6); and they *took* (as in Genesis 3:6) to wife such of them as *they chose*." God is not in the picture. Every man "chooses the good" as he sees it (Isaiah 7:15), without restraint, without concern to hear the God who alone knows good and evil.

Grasping hungrily for the proximate "good," humanity falls readily into the "evil" of hopeless alienation, with wrath and death as its final end. "The Lord saw that the wickedness of man was great in the earth, and that every imagination of the thought of his heart was only evil continually" (Genesis 6:5). "Evil" is now a moral term. The true "evil" in the world is not what people by their limited eyesight and judgment see and dread as evil. It is rather the commitment of human hearts to the wisdom of knowing good and evil by their own opened eyes alone, without hearing and trusting God. Desire and fear, passion and hate, each person calculating advantages with his own self as the center of reference; that is the force that animates all human conduct. The earth is now "corrupt in God's sight," and "filled with violence." Even the mark of Cain with its threat of vengeance restrains nobody who feels he may achieve greater advantage by simply ignoring it. The end can only be wrath, the determination of God to clean up the earth by destroying it and starting over. (Genesis 6:12-13)

We can hardly fail to recognize how vividly the society of Cain mirrors our own, both in its cultural achievements and in the symptoms of its alienation. Beneath all symptoms, however, there is the alienation itself, and this gets to be very individual, very personal.

## Chapter 2

# *THE FUGITIVE*

*Cain said to the Lord, "My punishment is greater than I can bear. Behold, thou hast driven me this day away from the ground; and from thy face I shall be hidden; and I shall be a fugitive and a wanderer on the earth, and whoever finds me will slay me."* Genesis 4:13-14

To be an alien means to be homeless, in a strange land, among people with whom you cannot communicate because they don't understand you and you don't understand them. The alien is lonely, friendless, isolated within himself. He cannot participate in or belong to what is going on around him, because he cannot identify or be identified with it. It is a painful business to be an alien whom nobody knows or wants or cares for, and whose most valuable contribution is to leave the natives alone and keep out of their way. Cain is the first instance, and the model, of the alien.

1. Alienated from himself. *"My punishment is greater than I can bear."*

Cain thinks about himself, sees what is happening to him now, and doesn't like it. Cain is sorry for himself. It strikes him that his act of murder has considerably more justification than the punishment imposed on him in consequence. Obviously everybody is against him. Nobody, not even God, understands him. There is a conspiracy abroad to destroy him as a person. Cain has no place to stand, no integrity of personhood sufficient to support him. If he is to have an identity, he must discover or create or assert it on his own. In spite of and against everything, he must justify himself by demonstrating his worth. But because the odds are so great against him, he feels he is entitled at least to pity from God and the world. Cain establishes a pity-fund, with himself as beneficiary, and makes the first contribution: "My punishment is greater than I can bear." Cain resists what he calls "my punishment." It is truly his, given him to be his own genuine possession. But he doesn't want it, and so he is alienated from himself.

It is a curious feature of all human language that people talk and think reflexively, about their own selves. "I love myself . . . hate myself . . . feel sorry for myself . . . am angry with myself . . . think about myself . . . could kill myself." Who is this "I," the subject of the sentence? Who is the "self" who appears as the object of the same sentence? Are they altogether identical? Not really. For the "I" is in control, the self is being controlled. The "I" operates by the knowledge of good and evil, even in examining that which it calls "myself." The "I" decides on the basis of what it sees, whether its "self" is attractive or unattractive, to be loved or hated. The "I" sits in judgment, the "myself" is on trial and receiving the verdict. "What right have you to judge me like this and speak this sentence upon me?" the "myself" might say. But it never gets a chance. The "I" isn't listening. We might ask, then, who the real person is in Cain, for example. Is it his "I" which protests the punishment and assumes the right to stand in judgment over it? Or is it the "self" which nevertheless must bear that punishment? Who is the real Cain? Cain himself could not answer the question, so alienated is he from his own identity.

I think of one late evening not long ago, when my wife and the older children were still up and the younger ones in bed. A teenage daughter began her lament. "You know what I don't like about myself?" she asked. And then she gave us a long list. "My hair is too fine. My nose is too broad. My ears are too big. My shoulders are too wide." And on and on. Most of that was the fault of my genes, I am sure. But then we began to answer. Her brother said, "Yup, that's right," and was ready to supplement her list out of his own critical observations. But her mother and sisters wanted to be reassuring and sympathetic. They dismissed her self-criticism. They brought out evidences that people liked her. They assured her that she was really charming, and assembled a list of her special talents. Psychologically she needed that supportive reassurance of her own personhood, of course.

And yet the counter-tactic of setting positive evidence against the negative does not really get at the problem of alienation. For the "I" is still in charge, gladly identifying with the self if things look favorable, but rebuking and standing apart from the self when they are not. The "I" is also capable of manipulating the "self," dressing it up as it were, in order to give it an appearance which will win the most favorable verdict possible from other people. Clearly, then, the "self" which is presented to the world is not identical with the "I" that dresses it up and teaches it its lines. Thus our very self-consciousness exhibits our alienation from our own selfhood.

The commandments of God offer a striking alternative. "You shall love the Lord your God with *all* your heart," God says (Deuteronomy 6:5). There is to be no heart or soul or strength left over whose energies can be diverted into judging the self, either to love it or to hate it. The verdict of the Lord God concerning us is sufficient, namely that he loves us and has made us his own. Similarly, the commandment which Jesus says is "like" this first, "You shall love your neighbor as yourself" (Leviticus 19:18; Matthew 22:39). When you exercise your "knowledge of good and evil" eyesight, get your own "self" out of the center of reference and put the "self" of your neighbor there! Let God be conscious of you, so that you can be conscious of your neighbor!

That, however, is more than we can manage. The wisdom of knowing good and evil holds us captive, enticing us with that next delightful opportunity, repelling us with that next fearful threat, so that we cannot stop thinking in terms of ourselves. We alternate between the heights of exhilaration and the depths of depression, between self-satisfaction one day and self-accusation the next. Everything depends on what we are able to *see*. We can see what we have done or not done. We can experience compliments and criticisms. We can estimate what people are thinking of us. We can compare our casual and accidental advantages with those of others. We notice it quickly when we get less in the way of blessings than others do, or more in the way of sufferings. These are the evidences on which we rely.

We do *not* rely on what God has said to us as by a voice from heaven in our baptism, "You are my beloved son with whom I am well pleased." The Word of God has value only when it offers calculable advantages. Cain could see no evidence that God's Word had value for him. The evidence suggested that the Word of God was not only nonsense but an insidious trick, an opiate whose only function was to keep Cain subdued and uncomplaining in the face of oppressive inequity. Cain invested his ultimate trust in what he was able to see. So do we all, for that belongs to the nature of man, and to his alienation from himself.

2. Alienated from the earth. *"Thou hast driven me this day away from the ground."*

In digging the grave, Cain has made the ground "open its mouth" to receive his brother's blood from his hand. Therefore, says Yahweh, he is "cursed from the ground," which will no longer contribute its strength to him (Genesis 4:10-12). The curse parallels Genesis 3:17-19, which projects a lifetime of toil, the frustration of thorns and thistles, sweat, and the inevitable destiny of dirt. Thus, when a man is determined to live by his "knowledge of good and evil" rather than by the word God has spoken to him, he finds himself at war with the ground. The outcome of that warfare is also decreed in advance. The ground will win.

It is not hard to see evidences of man's alienation from the ground. Start with his fundamental laziness, the willingness to be a bum, a parasite on the labor of others. Laziness, too, is a product of the knowledge of good and evil. For if life and activity depend on seeing something good and pursuing that, or in seeing something evil and running away from that, what happens when nothing seems good enough to be worth pursuing, or evil enough to be worth fleeing? There is, then, a vacuum of desire and fear, and what rushes in to fill it is laziness, a lack of activity born of lack of incentive.

The knowledge of good and evil demands that incentive be personally "relevant." "What's in it for me?" is the primary question. It does not seem very relevant to pitch in for somebody else's sake, let us say, for a mother at work in the kitchen. Again, what is the use of working if the labor invested is not likely to yield results sufficient to justify the effort expended? Such is the "knowledge of good and evil" calculation of the boy who believes that, no matter how hard he tries in math or in English, the best grade he can hope for is a "C." Besides, he doesn't like the subject, or the teacher, and cannot see that it will ever be "relevant" anyway. Even the fear of failure as an "evil" ceases to impress him. "Do you want to be a bum all your life?" his parents ask, but the threat is too distant. "Why sweat it?" he asks himself, in unconscious reminiscence of Genesis 3:19.

Add to laziness the dimension of alienation from people, and all effort becomes suspect which society in general associates with "cooperation" and "responsibility." If Cain goes picnicking at a public park, not only the personal irrelevance of cleaning up, but also his self-pity and anger makes him a litter-bug. "Abel's got plenty of time and money. Let *him* clean it up!"

In his divine humor God always manages to plant an unexpected and hidden curse in the good for which we strive by our own wisdom. Thus if the "good" is the freedom to be idle and not forced to do anything, the accompanying curse is *boredom*. "There is nothing to do," a child complains. The possibility that he may invest some time and sweat in the work of "tilling and keeping the garden" into which God placed him (Genesis 2:15) has already been ruled out as "boring." Equally closed is the possibility of serving under somebody else's command. That is "work," even "slavery" or "tyranny." So what is left is boredom. And what is needed is some kind of sedation, to deaden the sensitivity, so that boredom will go away.

There are many ways to escape boredom. One is to be entertained. We lose ourselves in contrived stories of battles other people are fighting, whether in movies, or television, or in story books and magazines. We expend energy vicariously, by watching athletes fight battles that only simulate life on athletic fields and in sports arenas.

But the drugging effect of entertainment as a means of escaping boredom is matched by the literal drugs—alcohol, drugs prescribed, drugs taken without prescription "for kicks." Add the mad obsession with the immediate and momentary diversion of sex. Add the perverse joy of groups sharing common resentments as they successfully withdraw from, and defy, the society that oppresses them. Add sudden flashes of inspiration for grand misadventure that culminate in destruction and vandalism. It is all a waste, a warfare against the cursed ground, for the ground is the enemy. It offers threat, not opportunity. It is hated, not enjoyed! But the ground will win!

There are other ways, however, of fighting the cursed ground. If the knowledge of good and evil can produce laziness, it can also generate activity. A man running madly from a charging bull is neither lazy nor bored. The fear of death exceeds the fear of work. Work is also better than pain, that is, if the pain is close and real enough to be taken seriously. The children of Israel as slaves in Egypt did respond, however reluctantly, to the lashes of their taskmasters.

On the other hand, the knowledge of good and evil can generate labor by its attractions. The possibility of earning money to buy something desirable, like electronic gear, or a motorcycle, or a car, may inspire a boy to work—provided the job is not too hard, and provided the returns also come up to what a friend is getting. Otherwise he quits. He will be nobody's "fool" or "slave." Sometimes creativity itself, the discovery of a capacity for achievement and the sense of fulfillment it offers, becomes the "good" to be pursued. Within its province, this is the most effective of incentives. It drives the student with the capacity for an "A" to invest the energy necessary to achieve that "A." There is joy and satisfaction in being able to do well, to dominate the earth in some area and force it, against its resistance, to yield its fruit. Every success yields a compliment, and that is a great "good," abundantly worth the investment of thought and labor. Unfortunately, not everybody catches or can catch that vision of reward. Those who do catch it drive themselves toward it with great energy and then look down with an eye of critical wrath upon any who lack such "drive," so wasting their lives and time in laziness and in escape from boredom. The higher anybody climbs, the more he tends to forget that he belongs to the earth, that he cannot really rise above it or set himself over it, that the earth will finally get him after all.

We don't want to think about that. The most subtle measure of our alienation from the ground is our fear and evasion of dying. The writer of Hebrews observes how we, for fear of death, are "subject to lifelong bondage" (Hebrews 2:15). The consciousness of death becomes a taskmaster, driving the alienated to prove themselves, to validate their existence in some way, luring them to establish some sign of immortal worth to which they may appeal against the testimony of the dirt to which they must finally return.

More than that, however, for fear of dying we absolutize life as the highest "good"—the kind of assumption against which Jesus warns when he says, "He who loves his life loses it" (John 12:25). It is one thing to value life as a magnificent gift and trust from the God who alone knows good and evil in the ultimate sense, and who is also the God of dying. It is quite another thing to love life in reaction to the mere dread of death. That is the way Cain loved life. When the horror of the body he had turned into a silent and bloody corpse struck home to him, Cain experienced an overpowering dread of being killed himself! He didn't know what to do with the life he had. He had lost all insight into what makes life valuable. And yet he was desperately concerned to stay alive!

The parody of that kind of love of life betrays itself in many ways. Our culture rejects any notion of a God who is ruthless in his wrath and judgment, any God who not only "makes alive" but also "kills," as the Bible portrays Yahweh (Deuteronomy 32:39). We somehow cannot accept the notion that the horrors of war can be willed on us by God, for God is "good" (as we conceive the "good" by our knowledge of good and evil) and does only the "good" things. Evil things like suffering and death can only be demonic, and it is blasphemy and escapism to attribute them to God. The term "act of God" is no longer applied to deadly and uncontrollable disasters—not only because our culture has become too sophisticated in its scientific calculation of cause and effect to believe that God has anything to do with it, but also because the very idea that *God* should "kill" masses of people strikes us as abhorrent and immoral. Capital punishment is increasingly rejected, I suspect, not merely because it has no deterrent value, but because our very dread of dying will not allow us to accept responsibility for attaching so ultimate a consequence even to the guilt of deliberate murder. The medical profession is the front line of our defense against our greatest fear, the fear of dying. That is why we honor it above all others.

But the ground strikes back and imposes a new dread—the dread of a deteriorating "quality" of life, of living and yet not knowing what life is for. In a world whose greatest wisdom is to know good and evil, we can never stop running. We escape one evil only to fall into another. The science of medicine improves world health and increases the span of life, but leaves the new problem of an exploding population. The science of agriculture yields new varieties of wheat and rice that will put an end to the threat of starvation, yet it threatens to send vast populations off the land and into the cities with nothing to do or to live for. The enormous advantages of technology and chemistry leave in their wake unexpected horrors of pollution. The security we find in setting power against power yields weaponry of mass destructiveness, not only of humankind but of the natural environment as well. We harness the oil resources of the world for the sake of power to the point of utter dependence, only to discover that our supply is depleted and that foreign nations control the flow. We develop technologies of gas and germ warfare, but do not know how to dispose of them when we decide we don't want them after all.

The laughter of the cursed ground, that is what we are hearing, and the sound of it tears society apart. Every time we achieve some "good," we find that we must run even harder, anticipate consequences more comprehensively, manipulate and control things even more wisely, so as to outwit the threat of some new "evil." Perhaps we enjoy the running for a while. The potential compliment of meeting a challenge courageously and imaginatively can be highly exhilarating. But when things get out of hand, when confidence falters, when the cursed earth laughs, then fear and sweat take over. The environmentalist's suspicion of hidden consequences is our newest, fear-laden tribute to an earth whose back-lash of curse is very real. Even the "experts" have failed us. We look to government for salvation, only to discover that government itself lacks the needed resources, wisdom, and power to save, but has ample power to waste, mislead, and destroy.

At the very least we see the god of science and technology falling from its pedestal. Our confidence in the power of the detached human brain to solve every problem by the application of more research, expertise, and money, has been badly shaken. A humanity which has set its hope in its capacity to "know good and evil" is discovered to be fugitive and wanderer still.

3. Alienated from God. *"From thy face I shall be hidden."*

As far as Cain is concerned, the Lord has turned his back and no longer cares about him. Yahweh himself, of course, has not said any such thing. This is simply Cain's own interpretation and inference. For the Lord did not hide from Adam and Eve, not even when they hid themselves from him, but confronted them and made them see him. Similarly, when the murder of Abel was complete, Yahweh did not allow Cain to evade him. Even when Cain is far off, begetting children and building a city, whether he knows it or not, it is his God who sustains him with all the good he enjoys and who delivers him from every evil. God has put his mark on Cain, after all.

Nevertheless, the alienation is real. "Truly, thou art a God who hidest thyself," says Isaiah 45:15. Cain can neither see God nor construct an image of him. God has ordained that men shall not know him by eyesight from within their "knowledge of good and evil" kind of wisdom. Cain is denied the privilege of examining God, poking and testing him as though he were buying some kind of product. There is only one way for Cain to know God—to listen when God speaks and to submit to him humbly, without subjecting God to dissecting criticism. Until Cain gives up on his eyes and learns to listen, his alienation from God must remain in force as the summation of the whole curse that rests upon him. But why doesn't Cain listen? Why didn't he? Why couldn't he? It would have been so simple, when God came to him, to throw himself on God, letting Yahweh do what he chose with him, trusting that God did not intend to cast him from his presence or take his holy Spirit from him (Psalm 51:11). Yet somehow so obvious and honest a thing was just impossible to Cain. That belongs to the mystery of sin.

"Then Cain went away from the presence of the Lord" (Genesis 4:16), driven by self-pity and anger, determined to pursue his rights and create his own life, seeking a place to stand from which to justify himself, impress God, prove himself right. God drives him on in that great adventure. "Show me, Cain! When you have created something admirable, present it to me and see whether it can stand the light of my face!" But God knows that Cain will not be able to win his approval or rise above the ground to which he belongs. "What is exalted among men is an abomination in the sight of God" (Luke 16:15). "Every one who exalts himself will be humbled" (Luke 14:11). That seals the alienation. The refrain runs through the whole Bible.

God is hidden from Cain, and yet he is so very close, if only Cain will know God as God insists on being known. Moses tells how close God is and how we are to know him in his sermon to Israel on the plains of Moab:

> *For this commandment which I command you this day is not too hard for you, neither is it far off. It is not in heaven that you should say, "Who will go up for us to heaven, and bring it to us, that we may hear it and do it?" Neither is it beyond the sea, that you should say, "Who will go over the sea for us, and bring it to us, that we may hear it and do it?" But* the word is very near you; *it is in your mouth and in your heart, so that you can do it.* (Deuteronomy 30:11-14)

God is as close as his word! There is no need to seek him in distant and exotic places. Recall from your memory and heart what it is that God once said to you! Recite it on your own lips! Take it seriously and believe it! Nothing more is necessary. In Jesus' parable of the lost son (Luke 15:11-32), the boy who ran away carried his father's word wherever he went, even into the pig-sty in which he finally found himself. Suddenly that word broke into his consciousness again. He heard his father calling him "my son," and he found himself saying "my father." That word, out of his heart and onto his lips, lifted him up, overcame the alienation, and brought him home. "The word is very near you."

Yet we want to be so wise. We dismiss the word of God as irrelevant and meaningless. Young people set off on the way of Cain, seeking a place to stand as though they had never had one, trying to see the face of the hidden God, groping for a selfhood they can admire and honor.

Where do you go then, you who want to be so wise? Perhaps you will try storming heaven! "Don't just give me words, God! Show yourself to me, let me see who is really talking! How can I know that this stuff is not just a lot of human opinion and superstition if I don't know first that you even exist? Come on, God, show yourself to me!" But God answers not a word. He will not defend himself, or argue his case before the eyes of those who insist on judging him. "The word is very near you," is all God will say.

Try again! "God, if you don't want to show yourself by signs from heaven, then show yourself on earth! Put a halo on the church to mark it as true. Make those so-called Christians shine the way they ought to, so that I can deduce the truth of your word from their sincerity and love. For they look to me like a bunch of pious hypocrites, interested only in the *status quo,* supporting the establishment, justifying themselves. I can be a better Christian without going to church! Don't you have to admit that, God? Isn't it true?" But God is silent. He does not show himself. "The word is very near you," the old, and yet ever new, word. Don't substitute your own judgments for it. Listen to it.

Then there is the possibility of a trip beyond the sea. Many in our day literally run away as far as they can in protest against an America and a Christianity they find intolerable, or to grasp for a culture the polar opposite of the western technological society they have come to see as a dead end. It is a religious quest, a search for a better ground. For Christian culture has brought forth and still nourishes the electronic mind which turns people into punched cards and numbers. The drive for "progress" has multiplied artificial needs to be filled by new products, and has brought forth the military-industrial-educational complex which sees nature and people only as things to be exploited. Surely God is not to be found there! Look rather for a world in which flowers and people are known for their own sakes, honored in the awe and tenderness of enjoyment! Look for a more authentic view of nature and man in non-technological cultures and in animistic religions whose practitioners were able to identify with the nature to which they belonged.

Still God remains hidden. There is a powerful appeal, to be sure, in the plea for a return to innocence and a recovery of sensitivity to nature and to people. Nevertheless, the old knowledge of good and evil remains in control, however radically man's perceptions are inverted. The science that had seemed so great a "good" is now seen to be demonic and "evil." The primitive non-science that had been judged to be merely superstition is now exalted as "good." But man remains the judge, even congratulating himself again on this new and greater revelation, and offering it as the way of salvation. The trouble is, it cannot save. Perhaps a handful of people here or there can withdraw momentarily into protest communities that have nothing to do with the technological establishment. In the end, however, the knowledge of good and evil demands its due. Men may fiddle with the knobs of their social and economic and political machinery, and now and then even design a new model. But they cannot simply junk it all and return to "nature."

A harder question remains. The Bible has been through this innocence thing before. It presents Adam and Eve as having been altogether within and a part of nature, able to appreciate and enjoy the fruits of the garden to which they belonged. And still they insisted on adopting the knowledge of good and evil, determined by their own eyesight, as their ultimate wisdom. *Why?* Cain and Abel were also refreshingly earthy in a pre-technological relationship, Abel delighting in his flock and Cain in the ground that responded to his planting. And yet, in so wholesome and clean and uncluttered an environment, Cain killed his brother. *Why?* Do we really resolve the problems of strife between people, of injustices and jealousies and hatreds, of arrogance and the desire to dominate, simply by altering environmental consciousness and summoning people to open themselves again to the reality that they belong to the earth? The summons is refreshing, and yet this strategy, too, is man's. Meanwhile God remains hidden. "The word is very near you," he says, and he waits for men to hear.

The search takes on still another dimension in St. Paul's paraphrase of Moses (Romans 10:6-7), "Who will descend into the abyss?" Let the abyss represent for us one more place men tend to seek God, this time the depths of internal selfhood, plumbed by introspection under the drive of self-consciousness. It is a genuine torment, this probing of the abyss within the self in the hope of finding truth or God, and its end is despair. When self-pity has yielded angry self-justification and counteraccusation, but no comfort, what shall a person do then? When the voices of guilt, rejection, loneliness, inadequacy, failure, boredom, conflict, emptiness and worthlessness refuse to be silenced, but keep raising their accusations anew through all the evasions and excuses, what then? Then something is needed "for the nerves," something to induce steadiness or forgetfulness—alcohol, or aspirin, or a cigarette, or a tranquilizer. Perhaps these can yield support for a moment, or an illusion of poise where there is none.

Further possibilities beckon, however, newer, more exotic in the hope and promise of diversion or discovery of realms of multicolored perception within the self. So now we have a vastly growing and attractive drug culture—marijuana, LSD, barbiturates, amphetamines—offering the possibility of a mind-expanding "trip"! Motivations vary from curiosity to rebellion to being "in" with a group, but all finally fall under the wisdom of pursuing or fleeing some self-determined "good" or "evil." It is a lie and illusion, of course, for the effect at best is to create pseudo-selfhoods in pseudo-communities. The abyss remains—dark, and deep, and potentially deadly.

Yet God does not want to remain hidden or alienated. "The Lord waits to be gracious to you," says Isaiah 30:18. "The word is very near you," says Moses. It is so very simple, if only you will start listening!

4. Alienation from People: *"Whoever finds me will slay me."*

That is the pathetic final cry of the fugitive. The fear of death is in it, but its form is the fear of people. Cain knows that he is under judgment. That's what "conscience" is all about. In its most fundamental sense, conscience is not yet the knowledge of what is right and what is wrong, but simply the awareness of being under judgment, looked at and subject to a verdict. We could live with that and even enjoy it, to be sure, if we could count on the verdict to be consistently favorable. Wouldn't it have been great for Cain if masses of people had gathered around to applaud him as their hero for wiping out Abel, their great oppressor, and setting them free?

Cain could delight in being under judgment if he could see the verdict swinging that way. But that is not what he anticipates. What he sees coming is the verdict of guilt, and with it the threat of retribution and vengeance.

Conscience, too, is a by-product of the knowledge of good and evil. At first we know good and evil purely individually, with ourselves as the center of reference, every man doing what is right in his own eyes (Judges 21:25). There comes a time, however, when "what other people will think" has to enter into the calculation. We become aware that our private calculation of advantage against disadvantage may bring us into conflict with somebody else's calculation. Now a new dimension of the knowledge of good and evil has come into play. People are judging us, rendering verdicts on us. To every other "good" we pursue, we must add this additional good, the respect and approval of our society. It is painful to be accused. The disrespect and contempt of people is an "evil" to be avoided at all costs.

Cain wasn't thinking about other people's opinions when he murdered his brother. Only after the fact, when the heat of rage and self-pity had been suddenly dissipated in violence, and when the bleeding and breathless body lay crumbled, motionless and silent before him, only then did he begin to think of death itself and of Yahweh, and of other people. "What have you done?" Yahweh asks, and the question is psychologically overpowering! "What have I done?" Cain has to hide the evidence! Till now he has dug in the ground only to plant crops. Now he must dig deeply to hide and cover over the body. When confronted with it he must also hide and cover over himself. "How should I know? Am I my brother's keeper?"

It was conscience that alienated Cain from his own self and from God. The final alienation, however, is from people. Cain feels that everybody is looking at him and passing judgment on him. Every man disagrees with him, hates him, and pronounces him guilty. Cain reads minds! All he can see in people's eyes is one grand conspiracy of vengeance. He trusts nobody, allows nobody to get close to him or really to know him. When anybody gets too close, Cain has to disappear, a fugitive again, like the "wandering stars" whose destiny is the "gloom of darkness" (Jude 13). Thus Cain becomes the image of all the fearfully self-conscious who dread people and escape the judgment of inferiority by hiding and withdrawing where nobody will notice them, reading every look as an accusation, seeking safety in not being seen at all.

But there are other reactions to the awareness of being judged. One may strive to do that which merits applause in the hope and expectation that the judgment may be favorable, complimentary rather than accusatory. The drive to "show them" can become a great power, standing in and alongside the dread of death as an impulse to make something of oneself and prove one's worth. Thus Cain's city becomes a show-piece of civilization, its culture and art calling for adulation from the society that had once rejected Cain. The drive to excel in music, in athletics, in beauty or personality, in authority, in wealth, and thus to gain the respect of people, has behind it the same basic conscience, the awareness of being under judgment and the desire that the verdict be good.

People who are driven aggressively to climb and make something of themselves soon, however, encounter another force. The same conscience that demands proof of worth also returns to enforce a "but." There are rules to the game and they must be obeyed. A gain on the football field is nullified and penalized if the rules have been violated. It is shameful to be found guilty and sent to jail. One demand society enforces rigorously is modesty. Bragging about achievements backfires, for the respect the achievement might have won is lost under the criticism of being "stuck on yourself."

It is a curious trap in which conscience places people. On the one hand there is the demand to make a mark and gain applause and admiration. On the other hand there is the demand to obey the rules and be respected as one who cares for other people. The first demand produces the great and driving achievers of our world, the second the moralists, whose greatest achievement consists of not hurting anybody. We may wonder seriously which comes off best. The aggressive hero wins the headlines. His very success makes his ruthlessness, to a considerable degree, pardonable. "Nice guys finish last," says the determined achiever. The moralist responds, "It's not whether you win or lose, but how you play the game." The moralist seeks approval in being decent and respectable. The trouble is, nobody notices him. He salves his conscience for his failure to achieve with remarks like, "I wouldn't want that kind of money." At least he is not accused and criticized. That, to him, is a great gain.

Both the achiever and the moralist (obviously the categories are not that neat!) have a store of social approval to fall back on in reassurance of their worth. They are likely to be reasonably at ease and adjusted. Abel had that great advantage, if we may stretch our story to think of him in such terms. In his prosperity he just did not experience the painful conflicts that fell to the lot of Cain. People would have looked up to Abel and found him pleasant, likeable, generous. If they needed a candidate for mayor or for the school board, or if they wanted advice, they would have gone to Abel rather than to Cain. For Abel, measured by his success, is obviously more important, smarter, and potentially more useful than his brother. That is the kind of judgment anybody, Abel included, would thoroughly enjoy.

Cain, on the other hand, may serve as our model for the people who cannot successfully compete. He always seems to get the short end. People don't ask him for advice, but keep offering their advice to him. Even in their efforts to be kind they become condescending, and subtly treat him as inferior. That, too, is a judgment, and it hurts. Cain curls up within himself, unable to discover in himself the kind of worth the whole world is so willing to confer on his brother.

Now comes another device people employ to escape the curse of being judged. They counterattack! Everybody knows that the best defense is a good offense. Counter-accusation, far more frequently than love (1 Peter 4:8), serves to "cover a multitude of sins." The accused becomes the accuser. The louder and more persistent his own accusations are, the less accusation he has to hear against himself. He can find sufficient ground to accuse anything and anybody —the establishment, the parent, the teacher, the police, the corrupt society. Soon the air is painfully filled with the cry of accusation from one side against the other, everyone dreading being accused and answering back in his own defense. For to be accused is a great evil, to be overcome at all costs!

All this is at work in Cain. He interprets the disadvantages under which he labors as a verdict against himself. His whole personhood is crushed by that judgment. He sees Abel approved, himself disapproved. His conscience cries that he is being judged, and protests that he is being judged wrongly. The word of God tells Cain he is *not* being judged, but Cain believes his conscience and regards the word of God as a lie. In his desperation to escape judgment, he becomes the judge and accuser of his brother, then his executioner.

Thus, conscience, by subjecting people to judgment, and by making them judges of one another, creates alienation between person and person. Life becomes a warfare, every man for himself. Other people are important in two ways. First, they are witnesses and judges who render verdicts of approval or disapproval. Secondly, they are potential allies or enemies—allies if they are useful toward achieving any desired "good," enemies if they stand in the way of that "good" or impose what seems to be an "evil." Aside from such functions, people are not really important. Even in these functions they are not important in themselves.

An alternative possibility in human relationships is described in Genesis 2:18-25. "It is not good that the man should be alone," Yahweh says. Notice that the decision here as to what is "good" or "not good" for man is God's. Adam doesn't even know what it is he needs, neither does he have anything to do with fulfilling the need. He is asleep when God does it, and when he wakes up there is the woman whom God has made from and for him. That is the beginning of society—a beginning that is celebrated anew every time one family yields up a son and another a daughter so that these two, in "leaving father and mother," may become "one flesh," a new unit of society, "not alone" anymore, but uniquely fulfilling one another.

The climax is the reference to their nakedness, without shame, before God and before one another (Genesis 2:25). The physical reality is only the emblem of the total psychological possibility. The man and the woman can be naked and unashamed because at this point they have no such thing as "conscience." They are not aware of being judged, looked at, subject to somebody's verdict. They are not thinking about being complimented or accused. The only verdict that counts is already in, namely that God has done a great and good thing in creating them in the world and for each other. "God saw everything that he had made, and behold, it was very good" (Genesis 1:31). That pronouncement is sufficient to make everything good, and no subsequent experience of testing can cancel out or diminish the force of God's prior and eternal verdict. So now, in the simplicity of conscience-less nakedness, lacking any thought of judging or being judged, able to enjoy the knowledge of God as the greatest of treasures and thus to receive and use God's gifts in perfect and uncritical confidence and thanksgiving, the man and the woman are able, fully and unabashedly, to receive and to know one another.

The world has lost that capacity, of course. It belongs to the unique wisdom of the Bible to tell us what has come in between—man's knowledge of good and evil, and with it, his self-conscious awareness of being judged. Until we are somehow delivered from that, it will do little good to press for physical or psychological nudism, or to plead for greater sensitivity to, love for, and acceptance of, people as people. All this may be ever so right in principle, yet the demand only leaves us the more under judgment, threatened with accusation, defensive. Hence we respond either by going into hiding or by putting on a show.

Cain is a fugitive and a wanderer in the earth. He is looking for a place to stand. What he comes up with is that little city, named Enochville after his son. Cain is the *father* of Enoch and of Enochville. Son and city derive their character from him.

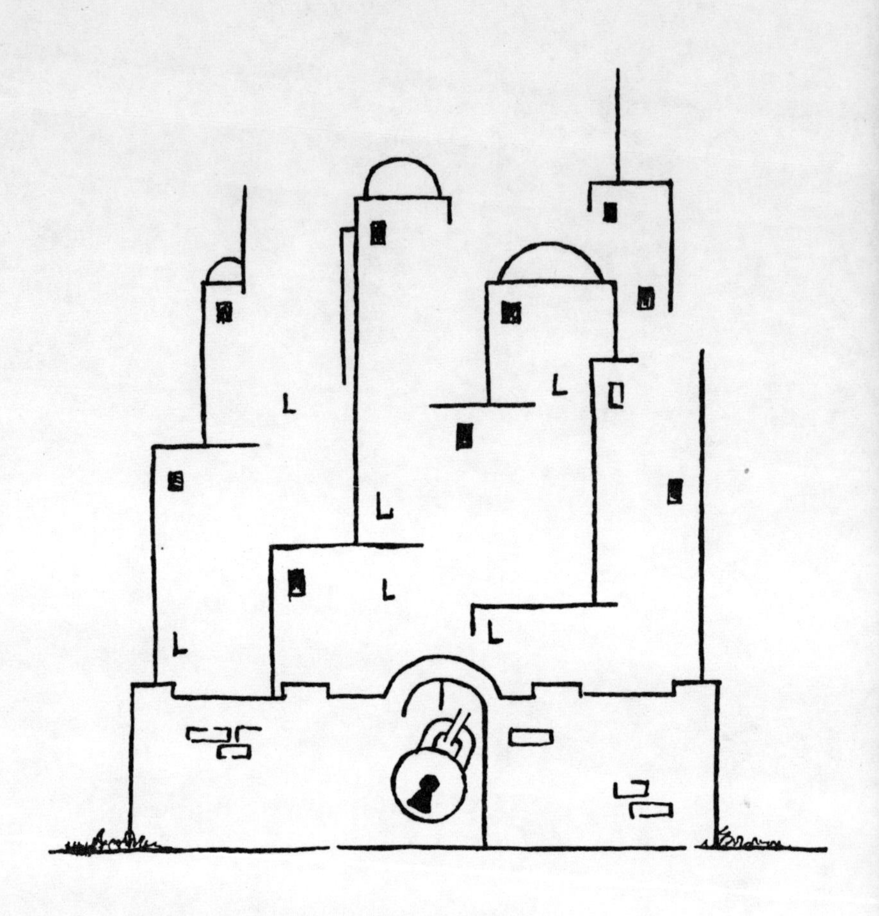

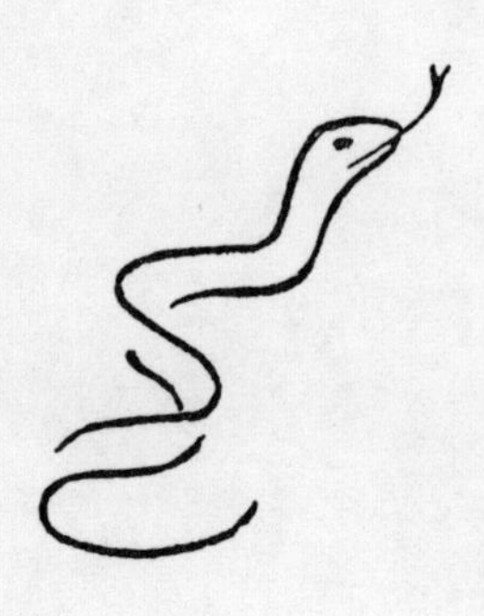

# Chapter 3

# *ENOCHVILLE*

*Cain built a city, and called the name of the city after the name of his son, Enoch.* Genesis 4:17

God was in hiding when Cain founded Enochville. No one would have dreamed that he had anything to do with it. It was Cain's work, built by the wisdom of knowing good and evil, the interplay of desire and fear that works in the heart of every man. Enochville had defenses of some kind, designed to give its inhabitants a sense of security against potential threat. Wall, ditch, watch-tower, something of the sort is commonly associated with the word for city. Let us think of it as a walled city, in order that it may symbolize for us the alienation of Cain, his suspicion and fear, his posture of defensiveness.

The founding of Enochville implies that Cain cannot keep running forever. He has to come to terms with himself, with the earth, with people. If no "place to stand" is given him, he must "father" such a place for himself, even as he "fathers" his son.

### Cain's Civilization

The holy writer respects Cain's achievement. Enochville symbolizes in embryo the pagan cities and civilizations he knows. He is ready to recognize as Jesus did, that "the sons of this world are wiser in their own generation than the sons of light" (Luke 16:8). For it was not in Israel that walled cities were conceived and created, but among pagan peoples who did not know Yahweh. Nor could Israel take credit for some of the most obvious instruments of culture—stringed and wind instruments and the arts associated with them. Israel was the borrower. So also with metallurgy and craftsmanship in iron and bronze, the creation of tools for peace and war. None of this originated in Israel. The people of God were always at a technological disadvantage. Even a posture of defiance like Lamech's, when he dared anybody to take vengeance on him for killing a young man who had wounded him (perhaps a classic instance of overreaction), would have been quite out of character for those who knew and served Yahweh. But Lamech's poem aptly defines the attitude of Enochville—defensive, self-confident, threatening, caring for nobody, ready to fight!

Enochville is Cain's answer to his alienation, a ground upon which he can stand. In this secular civilization he has created, Cain and his descendants can live with a reasonable degree of comfort, peace, and pleasure. They are capable of cooperation, friendship, and even love. Though father Cain is a murderer, he does not keep on killing people. The residents of Enochville are not murderers either, but solid citizens for the most part—decent, creative, and likeable. Though they live by the knowledge of good and evil, such wisdom proves to be generally workable. The citizens often wish that their eyesight could carry a little farther than it does, of course. It would be great to see into the future, and to anticipate every possible consequence so as to be able to adjust today's actions accordingly. They consult fortune tellers and astrologers in the hope of seeing more. They covet the higher wisdom of extra-sensory perception and intuition. They feed information into computers. They do not remember, of course, that Yahweh had foretold the future in warning to Cain when he said, "Sin is couching at the door," and that Cain had paid no attention. The only higher wisdom the citizens of Enochville want is one which *extends* their knowledge of good and evil. A wisdom which requires them to *surrender* such knowledge, and in obedience to God even act contrary to it, is foolish and unwelcome.

The knowledge of good and evil proves to be an effective instrument for creating a society. Conscience (the individual's awareness that he is being watched and judged by others) generates not only energetic works which merit approval, but also restrains public and overt violation of accepted standards. Furthermore, though each person judges what is "good" or "evil" with himself as the center of reference, there are common advantages to be pursued and threats to be avoided. These serve to bind people together in common causes. Conflicts are inevitable, to be sure—person against person, group against group, interest against interest. In that case there must be battle, but the winner has it his way and his way becomes law. Losers suffer what victors lay upon them. At least there is peace of sorts in a social relationship of winners over losers. The stratification of society is an inevitable factor in its stability. Many times, of course, the battle is fought without decisive result, to a kind of stalemate. Then the opposing forces work out a compromise and call it a treaty or contract. The contract becomes accepted law and is entered into the rules of the society. If anyone finds the law oppressive (that is, "evil") in its effect on him, he chafes under it and watches for an opportunity to escape the great evil and to achieve a greater good. This is the force that generates dishonesty, crime, deceit, and violence. The citizens of Enochville find themselves threatened by robbery, petty thievery, shop-lifting, rape, murder, the destructiveness of bombings, and arson.

Against such forces of lawlessness, Enochville must strengthen its gates and erect new walls. Its citizens invent locks, bolt their doors with chains, and install peek-holes to be able to see who is there. They buy guns and take lessons in self-defense. They strengthen their government and police forces. They enforce the law with courts and jails, fines and punishments. They create new legislation and tighten up the old. It is all very expensive, an enormous waste of money, energy, and anxiety, but it is necessary for security. Yet the process never ends. Those who seek advantage in subverting the law learn where the loopholes are. They out-wit the electronic eyes and the convex mirrors. They turn the law to advantage, and learn to purchase justice with money. Crime always remains a few steps ahead of the forces intended to control it. It continually increases, and Enochville's people are forced to find consolation in those rare moments when crime is found to be increasing at a slower rate.

### Justice in Cain's City

Enochville gives much praise to justice, and sets its hope in courts and laws. Nevertheless, every citizen understands justice in terms of the advantage or disadvantage it may impose upon him. Lamech's song is instructive. For Lamech, justice means two things. First, the community must concede that Lamach killed that youth in self-defense. It was really the youth's own fault. Secondly, the community must recognize how unfair it would be to take vengeance on Lamech. That would be the gravest injustice, worthy of seventy-sevenfold vengeance! The family of the murdered youth comes out on the short end of such a definition of justice, of course. They may feel that what justice really demands is Lamech's death. But Lamech, whose son has forged instruments of war from iron and bronze, occupies the position of strength. Hence, there is no appeal. The matter is settled; justice is done.

That's the way it is with justice. The best the little people can do is to press for *equity* of some sort, and to call that justice. On the basis of equity, they can press their claims for greater advantages. Justice is their great ideal, for it allies itself with their pursuit of "good" and escape from "evil." To the rich and strong, however, equity might mean some loss. Hence, justice means establishing their right to stay where they are. Precious as justice appears to be in Enochville, it requires courts. It needs the dispassionate verdicts of people who happen themselves to have no "conflict of interest," that is, no personal stake in that particular suit.

It is clear, therefore, that justice in Enochville is a form of accommodation to alienation. It does not achieve reconciliation. How can it? Cain resented Yahweh precisely because, in his sight, God had not dealt with him equitably. Anybody who has any feel for justice at all must concede that Cain has a point! Take Yahweh to court! Press the suit! Force God to act more justly, perhaps by cutting down on Abel's take and giving some of it to Cain. Abel, of course, would argue in turn that everything he got was his by right. Was it his fault that fortune had smiled on him? Since Enochville can think only in terms of justice and rights, Abel's attorney would argue that Yahweh's grace was not quite accidental after all. Abel had worked out a good arrangement with Yahweh through his generous sacrifice. Let Cain work his own way up and quit whining! The courts must then decree some settlement. But that settlement will not effect reconciliation between Cain and Abel, or between Cain and God. The "peace" it brings will be nothing more than an accommodation of alienation.

Obviously, the verdict issued in the name of justice must then be enforced. Once the line of law is drawn, nobody can be allowed, simply on the basis of his private "knowledge of good and evil," to break the rules. Law and its enforcement is Enochville's wall against any arbitrary and individualistic usurpation of power. That is what makes police, courts, jails, weapons, and even armies, so necessary. That is why these come to occupy so enormous a part of Enochville's attention, wealth, and energy.

It is really quite a trap! Indeed, the more intensively justice is pursued, the more aggravatingly injustice seems to be compounded! Citizens become concerned for their freedom as governmental officialdom invades more of their rights, all in the name of justice and security. Forced equity is suspect as being no equity at all. A campaign arises for an ideal greater than justice—love and sensitivity to people. How can justice justify the overwhelming curse and slaughter of a prolonged war Enochville feels compelled to wage in a distant land? A button factory imprints slogans like, "Make love, not war!" For war is a terrifying over-reaction. It degrades people to a status lower than beasts, and infinitely magnifies the horror of Abel's blood crying to the Lord from the ground. "Where have all the flowers gone? Gone to graveyards, every one! When will they ever learn?" That song was meant for the warmakers who claimed the war was necessary to keep aggressive people from cutting their detours around justice. The sensitivity people replied that the warmakers were in reality only nursing the military-industrial-scientific-political complex on the blood of Enochville's sons, as well as on the disrupted lives and mangled bodies of thousands of anonymous people in the arena of war for whom nobody cared! It was as though a "knowledge of good and evil" determined by the calculating *mind* was being subverted by another "knowledge of good and evil," this one determined by the *sensitive heart*. The result was, simply, new dimensions of alienation in Enochville.

How, then, can a truly humanized "civilization" become possible in Enochville? Some argued that Cain's city must undergo a thorough revolution. Its economic and social competitiveness had created inequities and ill-disguised slaveries. The establishment was both formed and controlled by the victors in such competition, whose first interest lay in preserving and augmenting their holdings. Losers were suppressed and treated like non-human machinery. The system of law and order had degenerated into a conspiracy to perpetuate oppressions. Perhaps if that system were broken, the oppressions would cease. Then people might find themselves free again, free of anger and hatred, free of ghettos and classifications, free of anger and hatred like Cain's, free to love and honor one another as persons.

But the governors and citizenry of Enochville were bewildered. They did not see how the city could simply dispense with its wall. It was not the wall that had caused that first and fundamental inequity by which Cain had viewed Abel as his oppressor. That inequity had come first! Out of that inequity came the protest and the violence of Cain. Out of it came the fugitive, and his fathering of Enochville! Alienated Cain was not the *son* of Enochville, but its *father!* The glory of Enochville was that here Cain could stop running, not because his alienation had been healed, but because it had been accommodated. What more can Enochville be expected to do? Here, at least, Cain has created a possibility of civilization, bearing the mark of the hidden God, in which his descendants can live together with some degree of stability, however tensioned, and even with some experience of joy! Meanwhile, the Lord God buys time and offers a hope for something better—for a reconciliation from the outside, a miraculous reconciliation, virgin-born, of which neither Cain nor Enochville can be the father!

Therefore Enochville's faltering and imperfect struggle to resolve tensions and to preserve a measure of peace by way of justice is a great gift, and not to be despised. Cain's city does not enjoy its alienation. It seizes upon every possible device to assuage the pain. It can appoint an investigating commission to conduct hearings in disputes like that between Cain and Abel, and offer mediation by an impartial third party. It may offer Abel police protection and put Cain under surveillance. It may promote freedom of dissent, so that the brothers have equal opportunity to plead their cases in the newspapers and on the television networks. It can provide opportunity for Cain to sue Abel in court if he thinks he has grounds for such a suit. It can prescribe psychological evaluations to get at the root of the hostility, and, if necessary, hospitalization and psychiatric care. Enochville can serve as referee, set down rules of combat, turn the opposing parties loose to slug away at each other with whatever authorized weapons may be handy, and stand by to supervise the signing of the contract when the contestants have fought to exhaustion. It can even encourage the brothers to try religion and go to church.

Or again, Enochville can deal with irresolvable inequities by coming to the aid of those who find themselves at the oppressed bottom of the economic pyramid. It can finance health and hospitalization for the sick, care for the aged, feed the hungry, support the jobless, and thus try to compensate for inequities it cannot overcome. When tensions rise high, it can plead for softer voices and greater willingness to listen on all sides. As an antidote to rebelliousness, it can urge greater permissiveness and relax laws which seem unnecessarily restrictive and arbitrary. Openness and tolerance are exalted. Raw rhetoric, though offensive and incomprehensible in terms of Enochville's traditions and values, ought to be heard as the voice of deeply felt protest, and not suppressed or turned off. Let society learn to meet change with patience and understanding rather than irritation. The era of long hair came in as an expression of protest against the image of acceptability perpetrated by barbers in conspiracy with school administrators. Unhemmed pants and dyed jeans were a protest against the clothier's projection of the neat and suave young conformist to the establishment. The appearance of unkempt dirtiness was a protest against the lies of greedy industrialists whose advertising seduced people into believing that the road to bliss is paved with soap, toothpaste, mouthwash, and deodorants, all on sale for a profitable price.

Thus Cain's city, always driven by events it cannot control, strains its mind and its resources with every possible argument and device to overcome the alienation so deeply rooted in its own character. Pluralism is a last, desperate answer, a confession that conflicts are beyond resolution. Everybody to his own life, to his own ideas! If these ideas are incompatible, then they do not really matter! What really matters is only that Cain and Abel not be so uptight about each other. Let Cain "cool it" with respect to Abel's advantageous position, and not resent the condescending superiority he senses (rightly or wrongly) in his brother. Let Abel understand Cain's anger, however unjust he may think it to be. But if they cannot understand each other, let them agree to disagree, for that is "civilized" behavior. Let them at least "respect one another as persons." For even if nobody understands anybody, and everybody ceases to hear, and all Enochville is weary of the argument and resentful of the need to assimilate what the dissidents are seeing and saying, at least everybody can agree that each person should continue to say what he pleases and that we shall all still be friends! Every mouth has the right to express an opinion, provided that every ear has the equal right not to listen.

Meanwhile, Enochville's debts mount. It costs money to have legislatures and courts and jails and police and locks. To wage wars in the name of justice is enormously expensive. To lift up the poor and care for the needy through welfare and medical aid, to help the disadvantaged and the jobless, to build the monuments to civilization which are the city's pride, to keep a show of peace when there is no peace, all cost money. Since the citizens run the government and make the laws, they can also see to it that the government does not take *their* money if they can possibly avoid it, but somebody else's! That is only good "knowledge of good and evil" common sense! Therefore, the debt of Enochville increases astronomically and beyond comprehension. And the interest rates increase. And inflation increases. And the economy staggers. And unemployment rises. And industries and cities begin to default on their debts. And distrust increases. The wise who see it coming devise strategies to take care of themselves. The helpless reassure themselves that the ultimate disaster will not happen until after they are dead. Every man for himself! That is Enochville's wisdom, the wisdom of "knowing good and evil"!

## Love in Cain's City

Then there is love. Enochville does indeed know and have a capacity for love. Decades ago, in a period of great depression, the city instituted programs of welfare for its poor which still go on. That was love. Then, after fighting a great war and defeating its enemies, Enochville loved them and contributed heavily out of its own resources to rebuild their ruins. That, too, was love. Again, when Enochville noticed how poor and underdeveloped lands far off envied its wealth and technology, it exported assistance and resources so that those who so desired could create their own technologies.

Before long, however, Enochville discovered that its love was not necessarily rewarded with love, but with resentment of its domination and condescending superiority. The technological assistance tended to benefit the few who controlled it, rather than the whole people for whom it was intended. Vicious wars were fought with weapons Enochville had created. It seemed that love generated evil rather than good, alienation rather than reconciliation, jealous suspicion rather than thankfulness, assertion of rights rather than respect and confidence. There are obvious problems with love in Enochville. Even when love tries to work, it does not heal alienation. What, then, is this thing called "love"?

Cain's city is capable, for one thing, of *attraction love*—like that which drew the "sons of God" to "the daughters of men" in Genesis 6:4. Jesus acknowledged the force of such love in Enochville. He called it love for "those who love you" (Matthew 5:46). It is good that Enochville has it—the attractions of friendship, romance, family, and good neighbors. But such love is limited. It lasts only as long as attraction and mutual advantage last. Then it simply ceases, as many a citizen of Enochville has testified who says, "I don't love him (or her) anymore."

This is a love both created and governed by self-interest, that is, by the knowledge of good and evil. Therefore it also strains against and finally breaks all bounds. Whatever memory Cain may bring with him of God's commandments, whatever residue of appreciation he may instill in his children for marriage and family, it soon fades. The wisdom of sheer desire, and the lust for affection and pleasure, puts tradition and commandment to the test and finds them wanting. If we love each other, why should we not have each other? There is no voice from God to give answer. Even the commandments, "You shall honor your father and your mother," or "You shall not commit adultery," ring hollow when there is no knowledge of God in the land. Therefore, the impromptu affair legitimizes itself while marriage is despised. Human relationships are not God-given. They are what people choose to make them at any moment. Lust conceives new and highly imaginative ways to fulfil its dreams. It preaches the good news of liberty and self-fulfillment. It justifies itself by the force of its propaganda and the numbers of its converts. In defense of its righteousness it parades as the new morality, depicts the traditional mores as a prison, prophesies that the family is on the way out and will give way to something better. But lust is emptiness and its rewards are dirt and death. Enochville's citizens discover that, but they cover it over with a great pretense of living.

Cain's city is also capable of *sympathy love*. This is a form of empathy, the capacity to identify emotionally with a heroic leader, or with a character in a movie or novel, or with a sports team, especially when it is winning. Sympathy love is the love of the strong, who, in the process of loving, gain reassurance that they are strong. By identifying with the weak, we compensate for and assuage our own fear of being weak. Sympathy is the love of the healthy for the sick, the living for the dying, the ones who have not suffered injustice for the ones who have. This is the love to which welfare agencies appeal when they put the picture of a crippled child on a poster, for sympathy love depends on some kind of "appeal," and a disabled or retarded child is far more appealing than someone equally disabled or retarded but full grown.

But sympathy love has severe limitations. It is unidirectional. Like water, it runs only downhill. The sick do not identify sympathetically with the healthy, or the defeated with the victorious, or the participants in an athletic contest with the spectators. When Cain is feeling so very sorry for himself, let Abel not come to him with any tale of woe of his own! "You think *you've* got troubles!" will be the contemptuous reply. Sympathy love rejoices in its own strength and in the recognition of it. Abel has little trouble loving

Cain when Cain is down. The white man can readily love the black when the black knows his place and acknowledges his dependence.

For Cain to love Abel with sympathy love would be to love uphill, and that is impossible. The inadequacy of sympathy love to overcome fundamental alienations is evident whenever you hear someone say in anger, "You will get no sympathy from me!" It can even become a game. Some people are able to make a good living by appealing to the sympathy of others. The strong learn to watch out for that trick, and not be taken in. Sympathy love is nourished on the rewards of appreciation and gratitude, and readily collapses when such confessions of dependency are not forthcoming.

Then there is *conscience love,* or love as a defense against feelings of guilt. Conscience is the awareness of being judged. It is conscience which rejoices in signs of approval and dreads disapproval. Conscience, properly invoked, can be counted on to drive the citizens of Enochville to greater diligence in the duty of loving. If the rich are made to feel guilty for having more than others, they can be seduced into investing not only money, but also time and effort and personal risk in social causes. Fund raisers know how it is done. They see to it that the rich client knows in passing what his competitor in the same bracket is giving. Then conscience love, a desire for the same appreciative thanksgiving and a fear of appearing to love less, can be counted on to bring the desired results.

Enochville has been forced to wrestle more than ever with her guilt under the persistent accusation of her lovelessness. Great prophets have appealed with passionate rhetoric to "the conscience of the American people." They have exposed a host of evident ills and injustices in the society of Cain . . . how the system of white-created and dominated politics and economics has been made to work to the disadvantage of the blacks . . . how the passion to climb and be somebody has had the effect of suppressing and crushing the spirits of those who, unable to compete, were passed by and ignored . . . how police and courts, often without realizing it, have consistently granted the white majority a quality of justice and favoritism which eluded the black . . . how the rich get away with dishonesty and oppression and are able to buy their way out of trouble while the poor are made to feel the fullest retribution of the law . . . how the majority-rule principle has operated to thwart equality of opportunity in education, jobs, and housing for minorities . . . how the paternalism of that perverse expression of sympathy love called "welfare" has degraded people and kept them in subtle bondage generation after generation . . . how the pledge of "liberty and justice for all" has become a mockery and joke for many . . . how it always seems to work out that the black man stands in the front lines of Enochville's wars in numbers all out of proportion to his part in the population . . . how the flight to the suburbs aggravates and perpetuates the stratification of society!

Arouse the conscience! Show Cain's city the shame of its injustices, and it will become more just! Accuse a president of making decisions only out of the cold calculation of the brain, without any "sensitivity to people," and pretty soon he will go out of his way to demonstrate how sensitive to people he is! Accuse the churches in Enochville of sitting around idly, comforting themselves with the sweet hope of heaven, blindly passing by the wounded man who was beset by robbers, and sure enough the church is roused by its conscience to love, to take the leadership in love and action and doing things for the oppressed, becoming the voice of judgment and doom and prophecy in Enochville.

Conscience is a great power! But conscience is also a precarious thing. When a man is attacked and made to feel guilty, his reaction is defensive, even when the activity that comes out is named "love." That fund raiser has to be a real manipulative artist when he approaches the client. He must drop the information about what somebody else is giving very casually, and then act as though he was not supposed to have let it out; if the client becomes aware that he is being made to feel guilty, or catches on to how he is being manipulated, the cause is lost. If Enochville's citizens tire of and begin to resist and resent the chorus of indignation and accusation dinned at them in the rhetoric of the prophets, and if their sympathy love begins to identify with beleaguered officials and a desecrated flag, then the cause to which such cries have sought to summon conscience love is lost. Alienation increases, polarization hardens.

Thus conscience love has no real power to overcome alienations either. It is a blessing in Enochville that such forms of love as attraction, sympathy, and conscience do exist. Yet all of these are still generated by and subject to the knowledge of good and evil.

They do not really transcend personal advantage. They may seem to shine momentarily now and then, in a forgetful ecstasy of total selflessness under unusual stimulation, but when the stimulation is past, the bridle of the self is discovered to be still attached. The father of Enochville is still Cain.

But if there should exist in Enochville another kind of love—genuinely free, non-magnetic, reaching to its object without attraction and even against repulsion, a love generated solely out of the character of the lover—the descendants of Cain would neither want it nor be able to comprehend it. For once the immediate needs of physical survival have been met, what people hunger for most deeply is the fulfilling evidence that they are worth something, and genuine love somehow provides no such evidence.

Let us suppose that Naamah, Tubalcain's sister, attracts a lover who tells her how beautiful she is. Since meeting her his whole life is transformed. He needs her. He cannot live without her! That kind of love makes her feel worthy, important, a real person! She revels in it because it compliments her! If Naamah should notice, however, that her lover's attention is diverted to some other girl who, Naamah thinks, is not nearly as attractive, she will complain to her friends, "What does he ever see in her?" or, "What's she got that I haven't got?" That betrays what the love is she wants, a love that *sees something in her*!

Pure, free, non-magnetic love isn't like that. Suppose a lover came on the scene who saw in Naamah nothing but repulsiveness and shame. Suppose he loved her nevertheless, not by any attraction but only because he was a genuinely loving person, and she more than anybody needed to be loved. She will hear no accusations from him, but neither will she get any compliments. She has no inherent beauty. It is his love alone that makes her beautiful and gives her a genuine dignity and freedom and purpose and hope. That is how God loved Israel when he took her to be his bride, as Ezekiel 16:1-14 graphically describes it. But will any citizen of Enochville want to be loved that way? To Naamah, that kind of love will appear incomprehensible, even degrading. It is humiliating to face the reality that she can exert no force of attraction, and Naamah does not want to be humiliated.

God's kind of love is foreign to Enochville. Its people are incapable both of giving and of receiving it. For Cain's city is not governed by love-for-nothing, but by its knowledge of good and evil. It is a city always under judgment—hungry for compliments, dreading criticism. If God visited Enochville, Cain would want to show him the glories of the town, but hide the slums. And if God happened to get a glimpse of those slums, Cain would be quick to say, "We are working on that!" Cain's goal is to make a great and favorable impression on God, to win a verdict of approval which will cover over the history of hatred and murder. When he hears that verdict, when God consents to all Cain's self-pity and anger and excuses, only then will Cain believe that God really loves him, that he is reconciled, and that religion is relevant.

Cain craves God's approbation so much that he turns the dream into a visible reality. He builds God a magnificent temple, brings sacrifices in great abundance, fashions a theological model of God with his mind or sculpts one with his hands. When God sees how much Cain has invested in worship, then he will surely agree that Cain is not all bad, but really takes God seriously and wants to do the right thing. Cain is comfortable with the god he has made. He sees to it that his god feels wanted. He hears his god saying all kinds of nice things to him, the kind of things Cain wants to hear. And now Cain sits back satisfied. His very prosperity and progress and cultural achievement adds up to evidence that all is well. For God, Cain convinces himself, has put his seal of approval on Cain's artful accommodation to alienation. God has conceded that Cain is right after all.

Yahweh in the heavens sees what Cain has done. "From thy face I shall be hidden," Cain had said. Cain would like to think he is hidden, at least from God the accuser, but here again he deludes himself like the ostrich with head in sand who thinks the enemy cannot see him now, like women in the locker room when a man's voice cries, "Close your eyes, girls! I'm coming through!" Enochville's eyes are closed to Yahweh; therefore the city imagines God does not see it.

But Yahweh does see the city. He sees everything Cain would want to show him—the art and games, the technological progress, the system of justice and law enforcement. Yahweh even loves the city. Though his patience with it is not forever (he destroyed it once with the flood), the mark of Cain remains on it as a sign that God has a hope for it and does not want it to perish. All of its blessings, the fruit of the ground, the enjoyment of pleasures, the satisfaction of creativity and achievement that makes further striving possible, the forms of love Enochville does experience—all are from Yahweh, even though Cain's city does not know it and Yahweh remains hidden.

But God also sees Enochville's wall. The city is built on a foundation of desire and of fear. Its compensations for alienation make civilization possible, but they do not touch the alienation itself. The fertile fields of boredom, self-pity, inequity, accusation, and conflicting desire continue to breed violence. The sense of futility and of emptiness grows. Progress is repeatedly exposed as self-deception. Wealth and freedom and pleasure bring only passing illusions of happiness. Youth fail to see purpose in what their parents are doing, and yet cannot discover an alternative which would give them sufficient reason to live and to strive. The city is rocked with problems it ought to solve and cannot. Every escape that is tried yields only more futility and deeper disaster.

Thus Enochville has not escaped the curse of Cain's alienation. It is founded upon sand. It is fugitive and wanderer still.

# PART TWO

# CHRIST

## The Word of Reconciliation

# *Christ: The Word of Reconciliation*

**Hebrews 12:12, 22-24**

*Therefore lift your drooping hands and strengthen your weak knees, and make straight paths for your feet. . . . For you have come to Mount Zion and to the city of the living God, the heavenly Jerusalem, and to innumerable angels in festal gathering, and to the assembly of the first-born who are enrolled in heaven, and to a judge who is God of all, and to the spirits of just men made perfect, and to Jesus, the mediator of a new covenant, and to the sprinkled blood that speaks more graciously than the blood of Abel.*

**Romans 5:6-11**

*While we were yet helpless, at the right time Christ died for the ungodly. Why, one will hardly die for a righteous man—though perhaps for a good man one will dare even to die. But God shows his love for us in that while we were yet sinners Christ died for us. Since, therefore, we are now justified by his blood, much more shall we be saved by him from the wrath of God. For if while we were enemies we were reconciled to God by the death of his Son, much more, now that we are reconciled, shall we be saved by his life. Not only so, but we also rejoice in God through our Lord Jesus Christ, through whom we have now received our reconciliation.*

**Ephesians 2:11-19**

*Therefore remember that at one time you Gentiles in the flesh, called the uncircumcision by what is called the circumcision, which is made in the flesh by hands—remember that you were at that time separated from Christ, alienated from the commonwealth of Israel, and strangers to the covenants of promise, having no hope and without God in the world. But now in Christ Jesus you who once were far off have been brought near in the blood of Christ. For he is our peace, who has made us both one, and has broken down the dividing wall of hostility, by abolishing in his flesh the law of commandments and ordinances, that he might create in himself one new man in place of the two, so making peace, and might reconcile us both to God in one body through the cross, thereby bringing the hostility to an end. And he came and preached peace to you who were far off and peace to those who were near; for through him we both have access in one Spirit to the Father. So then you are no longer strangers and sojourners, but you are fellow citizens with the saints and members of the household of God.*

Chapter 4

# *THE VOICE OF THE BLOOD*

*And the Lord said, "What have you done? The voice of your brother's blood is crying to me from the ground."* Genesis '4:10

*For you have come to . . . the city of the living God, . . . and to the assembly of the first-born who are enrolled in heaven, . . . and to Jesus, the mediator of a new covenant, and to the sprinkled blood that speaks more graciously than the blood of Abel.* Hebrews 12:22-24

What a contrast the writer of Hebrews sketches for us! Instead of Enochville, we have come "to the city of the living God." The "first-born" from whom this "assembly . . . enrolled in heaven" derives is not Cain but Jesus. No longer does the "blood of Abel" cry in accusation from the ground. Jesus, "the mediator of a new covenant," has silenced the accusation with his blood of grace and forgiveness and peace! "Therefore lift your drooping hands and strengthen your weak knees, and make straight paths for your feet!" (Hebrews 12: 12) This is not the walk of the self-pitying "fugitive and wanderer." This is the erect posture and strong walk of the pilgrims of God!

The contrast runs through the whole Bible. "Enoch walked with God," we are told (Genesis 5:22, 24). Abraham, while negotiating the purchase of a burial site, acknowledges himself to be "a stranger and a sojourner" in the land of the Hittites. But he is not "a fugitive and wanderer" in the sense of alienated Cain. Neither is Jacob when he flees to Haran from the anger of his brother Esau (Genesis 27: 43), or Joseph when he is taken to Egypt as a slave. The difference lies in the presence and promises of God. Moses did not mind being a wanderer in the wilderness, provided that Yahweh went with him. "For how shall it be known that I have found favor in thy sight, I and thy people? Is it not in thy going with us?" (Exodus 33: 15-16) The "favor" of Yahweh, that was Israel's unique gift and glory. God had called them to be his people (Exodus 6:7), and named them his "son" and "servant" (Exodus 4:22-23), and promised them an inheritance (Exodus 6:8). Therefore, wandering Israel walked with God. But Cain "went away from the presence of the Lord" (Genesis 4:16). Cain walked alone.

### Cain and Abel, a Figure of Gentile and Jew

It is not hard to see in the story of Cain and Abel a rather vivid figure and diagnosis of the animosity that divided Gentile from Jew, the nations from Israel. In the biblical perspective, Jew and Gentile are viewed corporately. Israel (after the Babylonian exile the focus is on Judah, or the "Jews") is the people of Yahweh. The nations (Gentiles) are not his people. These two embrace the whole of humanity.

Jew and Gentile are really brothers, both sons of Adam. And yet God has treated them so differently. For no reason at all, other than that he wanted it that way, God has had regard for Israel (Abel) and his sacrifice, but has disregarded the Gentile (Cain, symbolized in the Exodus history by Egypt's Pharaoh). Neither Israel nor Pharaoh, neither Jew nor Gentile, is more or less sinful or righteous, deserving or undeserving, than the other. That, as we have seen in our first chapter, is the inexplicable mystery. The question is, can Cain and Abel, in the face of such disparity of treatment, meet the test? Can they submit to Yahweh's will, wait patiently and trustingly until it unfolds to the end, and meanwhile cling to one another as brothers?

The Gentile world, as St. Paul depicts it in Ephesians 2, is formed in the image of Cain. "Wisdom" to the Gentile consists in knowing good and evil. The Gentile (like Cain) follows "the prince of the power of the air, the spirit that is now at work in the sons of disobedience." He lives "in the passions of the flesh, following the desires of body and mind" (Ephesians 2:2-3). The Gentiles are "alienated from the commonwealth of Israel, and strangers to the covenants of promise, having no hope and without God in the world" (Ephesians 2:12). They do not belong. They are excluded from all those precious advantages in which the Jews boast as the chosen people of God. Therefore, a "dividing wall of hostility" separates Gentile from Jew (Ephesians 2:14). And what creates the hostility? The Jew appears to be favored by God and the Gentile disregarded.

Abel, the Jew, knows it! It isn't only the Gentile who builds that wall of hostility. The Jews build it too! Latter-day Abel himself loses sight of God's free mercy, by which God pours out his gifts as he wills with no concern for what we think of as inequity. Instead of marvelling at God's grace, the Jew begins to imagine that his being chosen is a mark of his superiority. He interprets his advantages in terms of justice. If he is God's chosen heir, it must be because God has seen something special in him. His sacrifice must have been better. The Gentile nations, too, must have been given a chance to be God's chosen people, but rejected their opportunity because God's Law seemed too restrictive and burdensome to them! Somehow or another, the Jew thinks, his being chosen must add up to a recognition of his superiority and to a judgment that the Gentiles are inferior in the eyes of God. This is now a "fallen Abel," exalting himself over Cain. He boasts in the law he obeys, for it sets him apart from and over the Gentile. He finds perverse delight in the sins of the Gentiles, for they are clear evidence that Yahweh was right to invest his favor in the Jews and not in the nations.

Thus the wall of hostility grows. The Gentile, too, thinks in terms of justice and rights. He sees the fundamental unfairness of the Jewish claim, and blasphemes the name of that unjust God in whom the Jew takes such pride (Romans 2:24). He wants nothing to do with a God who plays favorites. Like Cain, he refuses to be inferior. He builds great cities and empires, and then turns his power and glory against Israel in devastating conquest—Assyria, Babylon, Persia, Greece, Egypt, Syria. Finally, it is Rome which holds Jerusalem and Judaea in humiliating submission. The world of Cain boasts of its music and art, its athletic competition and its philosophy, its technology and weaponry, its government and law enforcement, its success and its wealth. Many a Jew, awed and envious at all that grandeur, capitulates to his desire for what the Gentile culture offers, as the sons of God had done when they saw the beauties of the daughters of men in Genesis 6:2. In the era of Greek dominance, Jews in great numbers renounced their religion and heritage, for they saw no sign of their superiority or hope for the future in the way their God was now treating them. Notorious among these apostates in Jesus' day were those who turned to tax collecting and harlotry.

In general, however, the Jews still clung to their hope, some just drifting along, others aggressively pursuing it. They waited for the day of reversal and vindication, when Yahweh would reveal himself in glory as the God of all the nations, destroy all who opposed him, and exalt his son and servant Israel to his right hand as head over all kingdoms of the earth (Daniel 7:13-14). That day would reveal the kingdom of God, the ultimate projection and fulfilment of Israel's possession of the promised land. Then all the nations would have to acknowledge that Yahweh alone is God and king!

Toward that day the *Pharisees* kept themselves pure, urging all Israel to keep the law and not compromise their identity as God's people by contaminating themselves with the culture and life-style of the Gentiles.

An underground was also at work, ready to take arms when the occasion presented itself, and to follow any new "Joshua" or "David" into battle against the enemies of God. These were the Zealots, eager as Jehu of old to show their "zeal for the Lord" (2 Kings 10:16), knowing, as Judas Maccabeus had known, that "strength comes from Heaven," and that victory in battle does not depend on the size of the army (1 Maccabees 3:19). For when the Lord fights for his people as he has promised, then "one man of you puts to flight a thousand" (Joshua 23:10).

The wall of hostility was high! Gentile and Jew were enemies at heart, even when they lived together in stability and peace. They despised and hated each other. Each was willing to see the other perish without regret.

### The Visit of Yahweh

Then came that strange moment, small to the sight and yet infinitely great, which God placed at the very center of humanity and its history.

Out of Abel (the Jews) there appeared a man, Jesus of Nazareth. He came on the scene when John the Baptist had been proclaiming the imminent arrival of the promised kingdom of God. John summoned Israel to repent, to let go every attractive or fearful thing which might deter them from serving Yahweh only and from welcoming him when he came. As in the Exodus Israel had been marked as God's people by passing through the sea (1 Corinthians 10:1-2), so now they were sealed as God's people and heirs of the kingdom by baptism in the Jordan (Matthew 3:1-6). Now as then, it was not a question of status or rights, but purely of God's mercy (Matthew 21:31-32).

Thus Jesus also came, though from Galilee, to be baptized by John. There a voice from heaven, in words like those of Exodus 4:22-23, affirmed to him personally the full identity, hope, and calling of Israel: "This is my beloved Son, with whom I am well pleased" (Matthew 3:17). The Spirit of Yahweh also rested upon him, for Yahweh had a work for Jesus to do. Was all this an expression of favoritism? Did this name and Spirit make Jesus superior to his own people, or in and with them superior to the Gentiles? Jesus never thought of it that way. His task as the Son was not to have people serve him, but to serve them, even to giving his life (Matthew 20:28).

Jesus began to seek and to gather the lost and scattered sheep of the house of Israel (Matthew 9:36; 10:6). He did it urgently, for there was little time. The day of Yahweh was at hand, when the promises of God would be fulfilled to the people of God, but judgment and wrath would overthrow all outsiders and enemies who resisted that coming. Jesus sought out particularly those whose status within God's people might be in doubt. There were the Galileans whose blood-line had been compromised in past ages by mixed marriages and by the attractions of Cain's city. There were tax collectors and harlots, who had abandoned the hope of Israel and attached themselves to the life of the Gentile world for profit. There were lepers and blind and crippled and devil-possessed people, whose very disabilities testified that Yahweh "had no regard" for them. Jesus invited all these in freely. He lifted the judgment by pronouncing the forgiveness of sins and removed all doubt by healing those who sought healing and the kingdom. He prescribed no conditions, no probationary works. The ground of his gathering was mercy (Matthew 9:13), the stubbornly steadfast love by which the Father would not go back on his electing Word, or abandon even the gravest of renegades. The Father wanted them home without judgments of inferiority or accusations of unworthiness. He wanted them in on the kingdom. And the angels of heaven rejoiced over every one of these lost who repented (Luke 15:10), that is, who gave up his knowledge of good and evil so as to come home and live once again under the word and promises of God (Luke 15:11-24).

But there was trouble. Fallen Abel saw his superiority threatened by what Jesus was doing. The Pharisees and Sadducees (associated with the ruling priesthood) sent delegations to investigate Jesus. Where did Jesus get his information that the kingdom of God was coming? If from God, surely God would give some sign by which the responsible leaders, too, could be convinced of it! But Jesus offered no sign. He had seen no sign himself. He had simply heard the Word of God through John. If anyone knows God and trusts him, that Word is enough. Those who are truly "sons of the living God" (Hosea 1:10; Matthew 16:16) will not attempt to manage God's news, censor it, or calculate what advantages may go with believing it. "An evil and adulterous generation seeks for a sign," but then, when signs are given, still reserves the right to consider them inadequate (Matthew 16:1-4).

Well then, by what authority does Jesus receive sinners without subjecting them to the conditions of God's justice and law (Matthew 21:23)? In the case of the Pharisees, their diligent obedience testifies to their sincerity and the reality of their sonship. But Jesus lowers all the bars. He compromises the demands of the law, and thereby cheapens identity in Israel (Matthew 9:11; 12:2; 15:2). Jesus in reply quotes Hosea 6:6, "I desire steadfast love and not sacrifice, the knowledge of God, rather than burnt offerings" (Matthew 9:13; 12:8). Does religious work and sacrifice constitute a claim on God? In that case Yahweh abhors sacrifice, as all the prophets testify (Psalm 50; Isaiah 1:11; Amos 5:21-24). What the Father wants is children who are merciful as he is merciful (Luke 6:36). That is what the commandment requires, "You shall love your neighbor as yourself" (Matthew 22:39-40; Leviticus 19:18). The sick and tormented "sinners" on the fringes of Israel, whom the Pharisees treat with such judgmental indifference, these are like the traveler beset by thieves—wounded, stripped, and left for dead! The religious leaders of Israel see it and simply pass by. But Jesus, whom they despise as a "Samaritan" for his mixed blood and Galilean ancestry (John 8:41, 48), is at least showing the mercy of a "neighbor" to those who are so beaten and lost (Luke 10:25-37).

The anger of fallen Abel grows. What does this Galilean know, with his liberal and mixed-breed theology (John 7:32), and with his indifference to the law of Moses (John 9:28-29)? By what right does he talk so confidently about God his Father, as though he knows God and they do not, as though he serves God and they do not? Anyone can tell that Jesus is not God's son, but a sinner (John 9:16, 24), for he treats the laws of Sabbath and cleanliness with such disregard! He will enter the houses of tax collectors, touch lepers, let the unclean touch him, and sit down to a meal without washing his hands! For a sinner like him to lay so bold a claim to the sonship is blasphemy!

Most galling of all, why does Jesus not give the Pharisees the credit that is surely their due? Why does he not acknowledge that in the kingdom to come, those who have devoted their lives to keeping the law will have higher places than those who haven't even tried (Luke 14:7)? Fallen Abel wants compliments! He wants his superior achievements in religion to be recognized! For it violates the very justice of God that Jesus arbitrarily, out of his own wilfulness and in contempt for the law, offers every last minute repentant sinner a place in God's vineyard, and when the twelfth hour comes, a payment equal to that of those who have borne the burden and heat of the long day (Matthew 20:1-16)! It isn't fair that the renegade son who has wasted his Father's living with harlots and who ended in the pigsty, should get the big joyful party which returns him to full status of sonship with his hard-working elder brother! (Luke 15:11-32)

That is alienation! Fallen Abel insists on measuring things by his own eyesight, just as Cain did long ago! He cannot comprehend mercy, but only justice and rights. Justice is something he can see and control. He loves justice because in justice he achieves and preserves his advantages! It isn't right that God should be gracious to whom he will be gracious and show mercy to whom he will show mercy (Exodus 33:19). Mercy is altogether too arbitrary. The owner of the vineyard cannot be allowed to do as he chooses with what belongs to him. The eye of fallen Abel is evil and angry because his God is good (Matthew 20:15)!

Fallen Abel is angry as Cain had been angry long ago. God knows his anger, loves him, and warns him. Jesus himself goes to Jerusalem to be that voice of warning, for the kingdom is about to come, and Jerusalem, the very heartland of Israel, is the last to be ready to receive it. "Sin is couching at the door; its desire is for you, but you must master it," Yahweh had said (Genesis 4:7). Here now is the word of warning as it comes through to the latter-day, but fallen, Abel:

> *"You witness against yourselves, that you are sons of those who murdered the prophets. Fill up, then the measure of your fathers. . . . Therefore I send you prophets and wise men and scribes, some of whom you will kill and crucify . . . that upon you may come all the righteous blood shed on earth, from the blood of innocent Abel to the blood of Zechariah . . . O Jerusalem, Jerusalem, killing the prophets and stoning those who are sent to you! How often would I have gathered your children together as a hen gathers her brood under her wings, and you would not!"* (Matthew 23:31-37)

But fallen Abel is not listening. By every calculation of good and evil, Jesus must die. If Herod will not put him away, as he did John the Baptist, then the Council must. There is sufficient ground, for the laws against blasphemy carry the penalty of death.

The climactic opportunity arrives out of the threat of insurrection that swirls around Jesus. Zealotic enthusiasts hail him the new Joshua (or "Jesus"), the "son of David," the Messiah who will lead God's people in the final conquest that brings in the kingdom

(Matthew 21:8-9; 22:42-45). When God gives the signal, Jesus will know his role. Then the holy war will begin. Legions of angels will fight to overthrow the Roman beast and all Gentile tyranny. Jerusalem will come into its glory in the eternal reign of Yahweh! Here is another movement within fallen Abel! Men of violence are ready to take the kingdom by force (Matthew 11:12) on the day of divine vengeance against Cain!

But Cain (Rome) knows about walls and weapons and politics. He is ready to put down any revolt with utter ruthlessness (John 11:48), even if it means the total destruction of the temple, Jerusalem, and the whole Jewish people. Pontius Pilate, the Roman governor, lays it on the Jewish Council, under Caiaphas the High Priest, to keep the revolt from happening.

The Council meets, and Caiaphas' strategy comes through brilliantly in John 11:50: "It is expedient for you that one man should die for the people, and that the whole nation should not perish." Caiaphas concedes that Jesus is not guilty of fomenting insurrection. Nevertheless he is the key figure around whom the fanatical expectations turn. If he is put to death as an insurrectionist, the revolt will die. Under Jewish law he is worthy of death anyhow as a blasphemer against God (John 19:7). There need be no ethical compunctions, therefore, about arresting Jesus and offering him to Pilate as the one whose death will halt the threatened bloodbath and save Jerusalem from the fury of a misguided messianic war. Even for Pilate it is a good bargain. He will have kept the peace in an explosive situation at the price of just one life. Caesar himself would have to congratulate him for that.

Thus the plot is forged. Judas, perhaps desiring the kingdom to come and anticipating Jesus' glory and the intervention of angels, delivers Jesus up with a kiss (Matthew 26:15, 49). The disciples are ready with their swords for the holy war to begin, but the angels do not appear (Matthew 26:51-54). "If you seek me, let these men go," Jesus pleads (John 18:8). Thus he delivers himself up to the death he knows is coming. He is pronounced guilty of blasphemy under Jewish law, and the Jewish council delivers him up to Pilate (Matthew 27:2). In Pilate's court he faces a totally different charge, that of conspiring as a revolutionary king against Caesar. Pilate knows the charge is false. There are genuine revolutionaries at work, like Barabbas perhaps, and zealotic dreamers who want to press a crown on Jesus' head. But Jesus himself has even defended the payment of tribute to Caesar (Matthew 22:21). Pilate knows the real reason why the Jews have delivered Jesus to him (Matthew 27:18). Nevertheless, in the end there is nothing he can do except deliver Jesus up to be crucified (Matthew 27:26).

It is a remarkable scene. A great deal of Enochville-style "reconciliation" occurs in the process. Judas, the disciple, plots with the chief priests. He is as ready to use them as they are to use him (Matthew 26:14). King Herod and Pontius Pilate become friends, we are told (Luke 23:12). Even more significant, a mutual fear of revolt and catastrophic war reconciles Caiaphas and the Council (fallen Abel) to Pilate and the Roman authority (Cain). In that strange reconciliation of expediency the whole of humanity, Jew and Gentile, disciple and Herodian, gathers in common cause against just one man, the Son in whom God the Father has invested his name.

Thus the murder narrative of Genesis 4 is filled full. The drama is played anew. All humanity has been identified with Cain, over against one man. Jesus alone is truly Abel. Even now, Cain and Abel are brothers. Notice how the history of Cain and Abel is overlaid on the history of Jesus' death in 1 John 3:10-12. "By this it may be seen who are the children of God, and who are the children of the devil," namely, by watching who it is that loves his brother. "This is the message which you have heard from the beginning," that is, from the history of Jesus in whom the word of life was made manifest and by whom we have our fellowship with the Father (1 John 1:1-3). From this history comes the message "that we should love one another, and not be like Cain who was of the evil one (thus John 8:39-44) and murdered his brother (that is, Jesus). And why did he murder him? Because his own deeds were evil (thus John 3:19-20) and his brother's righteous (thus John 8:45-47). Do not wonder, brethren, that the world hates you (thus John 15:18-25)."

This diagnosis of the Jews (fallen Abel now allied with Cain) in their opposition to Jesus is significant. For all their outward concern for God's law, Cain's alienation had penetrated the Jews, too. Without realizing it, the Jews were limiting their obedience by considerations of human judgment, according to the knowledge of good and evil which characterizes "the evil one." They did not really want to know God's "truth," neither could they comprehend the freedom of full and genuine sonship (John 8:31-38). Sonship is not defined merely by physical descent. A son is like his father. What a son does betrays who his father really is! Jesus is the son indeed, for, as he says, "I always do what is pleasing to him" (John 8:29). Jesus knows the Father, trusts him to provide what is good and to deliver him from what is evil. He does not condition his obedience on the potential consequences. His deeds are, therefore, righteous. They conform to the very righteousness of God. This is what sonship means. But this is what the Jews found so intolerable in Jesus. It robbed them of all the advantages achieved by sacrificing. It drove them (like Cain) to the last resort of defensiveness, anger, and fear—murder.

### "One Man Should Die for the People"

The story of Jesus' death, however, ends not in alienation but in reconciliation. Caiaphas' political strategy that "one man should die for the people" was in reality prophetic, as not only John 11:51-52 but the entire New Testament proclamation recognizes. Surely Jesus' death did accomplish that "expedient" political objective. The revolt movement that had gathered its hope around Jesus' messiahship died in his death. For now, at least, Jerusalem was spared the blood bath that had threatened it. But there is more to the story than that.

This day, which we now call "Good Friday," was in fact God's Judgment Day. It was the day of Yahweh's visit, the day of the kingdom which John the Baptist and Jesus had proclaimed. It can be compared with that earlier day of judgment unfolded in Genesis 6, when the whole of humanity had been corrupted with the sin of Cain. God resolved then to destroy the earth and to begin again with just one man, Noah. And he did! Now the earth faces its final crisis. The day of the kingdom is here, when Israel should inherit and enter the kingdom of God, and all the kingdoms of sin and corruption should perish. But where is Israel? They have all gone over to the side of Cain! God is not deceived by their religion. He knows their hearts (Luke 16:15)! What essential difference does it make if Gentile kings seek worth and glory by conquest, or if greedy men seek it in wealth, or if lustful men seek it through the passions of their flesh, or if a self-pitying and suppressed people seek vindication and superiority through the works of religion? As Psalm 14:3 puts it, "They have all gone astray, they are all alike corrupt; there is none that does good, no, not one."

Who then shall receive the kingdom? At the Father's right hand, from the entire flock of his people, is found only one little lamb, Jesus. Shall Yahweh go through with his judgment, destroy the ungodly, and give the kingdom to just that one? God's heart "recoils" within him, and Hosea 11:8-9 unfolds the decision. "I will not execute my fierce anger . . . for I am God and not man, the Holy One in your midst, and I will not come to destroy." The Father speaks to his Son, and the Son answers, "Not as I will, but as thou wilt" (Matthew 26:39). Jesus stands in the breach (Psalm 106:23; Ezekiel 22:30). He drinks the cup of the wine of the wrath of God, which has been poured out for Jerusalem and for all the nations (Jeremiah 25:15-29; Matthew 26:36-46; Mark 10:38; John 18:11). "Like a lamb that is led to the slaughter, . . . so he opened not his mouth" (Isaiah 53:7). This is the Lord's Day of judgment and of salvation. "It is marvelous in our eyes" (Psalm 118:23; Matthew 21:42).

Jesus' resurrection proclaimed what the Father had really been doing. Without the resurrection the disciples could not escape their wisdom of knowing good and evil, as they saw things with their own eyes. They could only infer that God was dead after all. Surely the living God, if there were one, could not let his one faithful Son die at the hands of wicked men! "God forbid, Lord! This shall never happen to you," Peter had said (Matthew 16:22). As for those who had plotted the death for the sake of expediency and judged Jesus the blasphemer, they now had all the necessary proof that they were right. His trust in God, his claim to be the Son of God, it was all a lie, just as his kingship was a lie (Matthew 27:39-44). The evidence shouts that God has forsaken him. Jesus has deluded not only the people, but also himself. He said the kingdom was coming and it did not come!

Then comes the third day. The grave is empty. Jesus stands alive among his disciples. The promise spoken by his Father comes true,

"After two days I will revive you; on the third day I will raise you up, that you may live before me" (Hosea 6:2, paraphrased). The last word is spoken not by darkness and death, but by resurrection and life. Therefore, the disciples cannot be left in their guilt, despair, and fear. It is a day of joy and of peace. The Son, who trusted and served his Father even to death, inherits the kingdom at God's right hand, but not for himself alone. There are many rooms in his Father's house, eager for occupancy, reservations made (John 14:2; 1 Peter 1:4). Jesus lives, not to gloat over his enemies nor to vindicate himself by a display of glorious revenge, but to win back to God the world whose reprieve has been bought by his dying.

### Reconciliation

The world stands, mankind survives, because in the critical moment that one man died. This is the reconciliation and atonement which the New Testament celebrates in so many great texts. "While we were yet helpless, at the right time Christ died for the ungodly" (Romans 5:6). "God was in Christ reconciling the world to himself . . . For our sake he made him to be sin who knew no sin" (2 Corinthians 5:18, 21). "He has appeared once for all at the end of the age to put away sin by the sacrifice of himself" (Hebrews 9:26). "Thou wast slain and by thy blood didst ransom men for God from every tribe and tongue and people and nation" (Revelation 5:9).

What it all means is that Cain can come home. He can put his fear and anger aside, tear down his wall, surrender Enochville to Yahweh. The blood of Abel his brother is not crying against him any more. Cain, with all the saints whom God has loved, can "come to Mount Zion and to the city of the living God, the heavenly Jerusalem . . . and to the assembly of the first-born . . . and to Jesus . . . and to the sprinkled blood that speaks more graciously than the blood of Abel" (Hebrews 12:22-24).

For God has turned mankind's ultimate act of alienation and murder into forgiveness and peace for the sake of the murderers! The uncleanest of sacrifices, offered for the sake of expediency on the hill of the skull, has been accepted by God as the end of all sacrificing. Cain and fallen Abel brought this sacrifice together. Nor did they take it from the produce of field or flock. It was their own brother. But Yahweh, for no reason at all other than his incomprehensible goodness, grace, and mercy (Exodus 33:18-20), "had regard for" that scandalous sacrifice and for those who offered it. Do you see it now, Cain? You could not trust yourself to Yahweh's mercy before. When you saw how unequally God treated you, what blessings Abel received and what burdens you were given to bear, you became angry. You pitied yourself, hated your brother, and killed him. But now look at Jesus! He trusted Yahweh's mercy even to the death, even when he was stripped naked of everything you thought was so important! And he did not emerge the loser. "God has highly exalted him and bestowed on him the name which is above every name" (Philippians 2:9).

Open your eyes, Cain, and see the truth! You did it! Now eat it! Get in on that sacrifice by eating it! (1 Corinthians 10:18) Horrible thought! Can you imagine eating the flesh and drinking the blood of Abel, whom you killed and buried in the ground? But this blood is different. It does not condemn you, but offers you life! "He who eats my flesh and drinks my blood has eternal life" (John 6:54). Eat it and drink it! It is the body given for you, the blood shed for you to forgive your sins and restore you to the family of God (Matthew 26:26-28). This blood condemns not you, but only the "sin in the flesh" that ambushed you (Romans 8:3; Genesis 4:7). No accusations against you can stand, for Jesus your brother at Yahweh's right hand is pleading *for* you, not against you (Romans 8:1, 31-34). You didn't know it, but while you were yet a sinner, Christ died for you. "While we were enemies we were reconciled to God by the death of his Son" (Romans 5:8-10). Come home, Cain! See Jesus your brother, alive and well, offering nothing but peace!

That is the reconciliation. It unites not only Cain and Yahweh, but also Cain and Abel as brothers. The wall of hostility that divided them is broken down (Ephesians 2:14). They have been discovered in a common guilt, and yet delivered together from the wrath that should have destroyed them both. Let not the Gentile boast of his great civilization, or the Jew of his ancestry, circumcision, and obedience to the law. They have nothing to present to God now, save their bloody hands. They have no excuse, no defense against their blood-guilt, and no hope—except that by God's miracle of eternal mercy, the very blood they shed is returned to them for their cleansing. That is why the Gentiles can no longer be excluded as aliens. The world, all humanity, died and rose again in Jesus' death and resurrection. For Jew or for Gentile, the only thing that matters now is what God did in Christ. "But now in Christ Jesus you who once were far off have been brought near in the blood of Christ. For he is our peace, who has made both one (Jew and Gentile, Abel and Cain), and has broken down the dividing wall of hostility . . . And he came and preached peace to you who were far off and peace to those who were near; for through him we both have access in one Spirit to the Father." (Ephesians 2:13-18) That is the reconciliation!

**Jesus, the Reconciler**

This reconciliation is not a matter of psychological experience or philosophical insight. It is rooted in a person and an event, that is, in the personal history of Jesus of Nazareth. To know the reconciliation and its power more fully, we need to recognize what was so different and unique about him.

Jesus lived by the "wisdom" of the man he describes in Matthew 7:24-25, who "built his house," not on "the sand" of Enochville's knowledge of good and evil, but on "the rock" of his Father's word and promises. He heard and understood what the Father was saying to him and to Israel. He trusted and lived by that word against temptation, against the evidence of defeat, against accusation and threat, against death and the cross. For the sake of God's promise he gave up every treasure he had (Matthew 13:44-45). When he suffered, as St. Peter remembers it (1 Peter 2:23), he did not respond in threat and anger. All the evidence screamed that God had disregarded him and his sacrifice, and blessed with success and prosperity the sacrifices of Caiaphas' temple. Pain, shame, and the total unfairness of it all testified loudly that God had forsaken him! But Jesus clung to God's promise. "You are my beloved son! You are my servant! You are my heir! You will have the kingdom! Death will not destroy you! On the third day I will raise you up, that you may live before me." Thus Jesus was not alienated from God as Cain was, even when it seemed that God had hidden his face from him.

Neither was Jesus alienated from the earth. He did not fear the earth, nor assert his independence of, or superiority over it. He was ready to return to its dust, to be nailed to a cross made from a tree out of that earth.

Neither was Jesus alienated from people. He was isolated by his enemies, it is true, and abandoned even by his disciples. He was alone, as he says in John 16:32, except that the Father did not leave him alone. And yet Jesus was not alienated from people, not even from his enemies, for he acknowledged no barrier between himself and them. The people were not the enemy, after all. The enemy was the seven devils who had entered the house of Jesus' countrymen to dwell there, making their last state worse than the first (Matthew 12:43-45). Jesus saw how Satan "demanded to have" Peter and the disciples, even as sin, couching at the door, had desired to have Cain (Luke 22:31). Sin, death, Satan, the impending wrath and judgment of God, that was the enemy to be overcome, not people. That is why Jesus died in love and patience, without a word of vituperation. He died, rather, with the prayer that the Father would keep the disciples through their crisis (John 17:15) and forgive even his enemies, "for they know not what they do" (Luke 23:34).

Nor was Jesus alienated from himself. He still knew who he was. Hence there was no self-pity, no complaint like Cain's that the punishment was greater than he could bear. His eye was not on himself, but on the people he loved, on the Jerusalem he did not want destroyed, and on the Father whose promise he trusted and into whose hands he committed his spirit (Luke 23:46).

In Jesus we see what it is like to stand before God without alienation, and before men with love. Jesus' love was beyond attraction, beyond sympathy, beyond conscience. It was the love of one who, breathing the Spirit of God, possessed the Father's own mind and character. He did not resist or try to manipulate God, but simply trusted and served him in extending God's mercy to an alienated world. His Father did not leave him destitute and ashamed, holding an empty bag. Jesus gained the victory, not for himself only but for the very humanity which had conspired to crucify him.

If the reconciliation God now offers to alienated Cain and to fallen Abel appears to be very foolish, that is exactly God's intention. By it God destroys the wisdom of the wise and thwarts the cleverness of the clever, as St. Paul says, "for the foolishness of God is wiser than men, and the weakness of God is stronger than men" (1 Corinthians 1:19, 25). If you want to know me, God is saying, don't bother to explore the heights of heaven or the depths of earth (Romans 10:6-7). Just open your ears and listen. For my word is very near you. It addresses you out of the person and event of Jesus Christ, crucified and risen again (John 1:14; Revelation 19: 13). If you are serious about wanting to know me, then come to terms with what you did, and what Jesus did, and what I did, in that cross. Do you want to see my glory (Exodus 33:17-20), the promised glory of Yahweh himself (Isaiah 40:5)? Then don't look for visible demonstrations of a glory which you can evaluate on the basis of your distorted wisdom. Let my glory shine into the darkness of your heart, to give you "the light of the knowledge of the glory of God in the face of Christ" (2 Corinthians 4:5). He alone is "the way" by which you come to me (John 14:6).

The wise world doesn't like it. The event is too small, the cross too degrading, baptismal water too foolish. But God does not back down. In the wisdom of God, the world shall not know God through wisdom, St. Paul says, but "through the folly of what we preach," for "God chose what is foolish in the world to shame the wise, God chose what is weak in the world to shame the strong" (1 Corinthians 1:21, 27). Let the wise man become a fool, if he wants to be truly wise. The great must become small to enter the Kingdom of God, as small as little children (Matthew 18:3), small enough even to re-enter the womb and be born again (John 3:3-6), small enough to pass through the eye of a needle (Matthew 19:24).

"Let not the wise man glory in his wisdom, let not the mighty man glory in his might, let not the rich man glory in his riches; but let him who glories glory in this, that he understands and knows me, that I am the Lord who practices kindness, justice, and righteousness in the earth; for in these things I delight, says the Lord" (Jeremiah 9:23-24). What a difference that would make in the relationship between Cain and Abel! If the brothers understand and know Yahweh, then they will believe against sight that Yahweh "practices kindness, justice, and righteousness in the earth" even when he treats them so differently. Abel will not glory in his riches,

Cain will not feel bitter and inferior in his poverty. For the glory of both is to know Yahweh! The brothers stand together on that one rock, each accepting the uniqueness of his life and calling, each with his eye on Yahweh, neither comparing himself with the other. Each possesses a perfect and complete selfhood which God created and loves. No experience of prosperity or adversity can detract from that selfhood, nor add to it. Therefore, Cain and Abel can love and honor one another, without shame or jealousy on the one side, without pride or condescension on the other. In the open freedom of their mutual trust and honor, they can share what they have in giving and receiving, seek God's will for them individually and together, and wait patiently for God to make clear his purposes.

**Wanderers No More**

Now that is what God offers to the world in the cross and resurrection of Christ. "We beseech you on behalf of Christ, *be reconciled to God*" (2 Corinthians 5:19-20). Reconciliation begins with God. In baptism God speaks to us the words of the voice from heaven, "You are my beloved son, my heir, my servant!" That word stands forever, independent of all evidence, proof against all accusation. It lifts us up when we fall into depression and despair, and brings us down when we imagine we are important because we have done or experienced something the world applauds or envies. For only one treasure matters. "This is eternal life," Jesus says, "that they know thee the only true God, and Jesus Christ whom thou hast sent" (John 17:3).

And so we are *reconciled also to our own selfhood.* We are not in the business of judging ourselves any more (1 Corinthians 4:4). The Lord's judgment is in, and that is all that matters. Nothing can add to or detract from that. See it in the exuberant confession of St. Paul, how all his evident experiences, including the criticisms and judgments of men, cannot really touch him.

> *We are treated as impostors, and yet are true; as unknown, and yet well known; as dying and behold we live; as punished, and yet not killed; as sorrowful, yet always rejoicing; as poor, yet making many rich; as having nothing, and yet possessing everything.* (2 Corinthians 6:8-10)

There is no fear of loss here, no self-estrangement. If only Cain could have said something like that; "I am mistreated, and yet well-treated; overlooked, yet not forgotten; made the least, yet losing no status; beneath my brother, yet my brother's keeper."

Show that to young people who fight their desperate battles of self-consciousness, afraid both of being noticed and of being not noticed, suspicious and angry at being treated like a number on a punched computer card, a statistic, a faceless nobody in the mass of indifferent humanity, ready to cry out, "I am a person! Do not fold, tear, mutilate, or spindle!"

God answers, "Relax! People don't make you a person, I do. No opposition or indifference or irritation or accusation or demands of men can take that from you. You are my son and heir! Never for a moment are you hidden from or forgotten by me. For my mind is greater than yours. People have to classify and group you, in order to think. They see the lawn, but I see every blade of grass. People see a head of hair, but before me every hair of your head is numbered. Your selfhood is not determined by what happens to you, or touched by the way people judge, classify, mis-classify, or ignore you. You have your selfhood from me. Take it, and use it. No loneliness or fear of worthlessness, no accusation, no shame and guilt, no sense of inadequacy or purposeless drift can hurt you, or thwart what I am doing with that life of yours, or dim the glory I have invested in you."

By that same word of God we find ourselves *reconciled also to the earth.* In the resurrection of Christ, even the dread of death is broken (1 Corinthians 15:55-57). Death does not have the last word after all. The fear men invest in death ought much more properly to be invested in their God (Matthew 10:28). We are willing to be dust and to return to the dust. Life does not demand proof that we are more than dirt. No longer do we have to pervert our dominion over the earth in the illusion that our success in being creative and in making the earth and people dance to our tune makes us worth something. We are not deceived by the myth of scientific and technological progress. The good our eye sees and desires is no ultimate good; therefore we are not driven to pay the price of destroying the earth in order to have it. The evil our eye sees is not the ultimate evil; therefore we are under no desperate compulsion to create the ultimate in technological weapons of destruction in order to deliver ourselves.

So we can honor the earth to which we belong and treat it tenderly and appreciatively as a gift of God, exercising our God-given dominion as a trust from him without arrogance and without abuse. We can unabashedly enjoy its fruits and its beauties as God chooses to pour them out upon us, and in that enjoyment, share them with our neighbors.

Finally, we are *reconciled to people.* Enochville's wall of fear and resentment cannot exclude the radiation of love that proceeds from Calvary. No barrier men erect can prohibit such fruits of the Spirit as "love, joy, peace, patience, kindness, goodness, faithfulness, gentleness, self-control." "Against such there is no law," St. Paul adds (Galatians 5:22), that is, no wall.

That is the beauty of reconciliation. A love is at work which blithely ignores obstacles, bears hatred and rebuff with good cheer, and transcends all human measurements and stratifications. "From a human point of view" (2 Corinthians 5:16) in the competitive culture of Cain's city, it may seem advantageous to be white rather than black, rich rather than poor, at the top rather than at the bottom, slim rather than fat, popular rather than ignored, victorious rather than defeated. Those who belong to the "new creation" in Christ, however, recognize that "the new has come" (2 Corinthians 5:17). They see God pouring out his gifts in infinite variety, without concern for what human calculation would call "equality." They see God measuring all men solely by the one love in which he created them, and the one redemption by which he reconciled the world of alienated humanity to himself. In that vision, the command to "love your neighbor as yourself" is not just theory any more. For if God promises to give his children every good and to deliver them from evil, those who are his sons need no longer keep themselves at the anxious center of their calculation. They can put their neighbor in that center, press the question of good and evil with reference to him, act accordingly, and entrust the consequence of blessing to God.

Cain and Abel have been given a common place to stand. Cain's is not a valley of depression, and Abel's is not a mountain of superiority. They stand together on the one word of God which names them both son and heir, servants of a single divine purpose. They are brothers. As brothers they trust their one Father, receive their varied gifts with thanksgiving, lift their eyes to God in one hope, and share themselves in free generosity with one another and with their world.

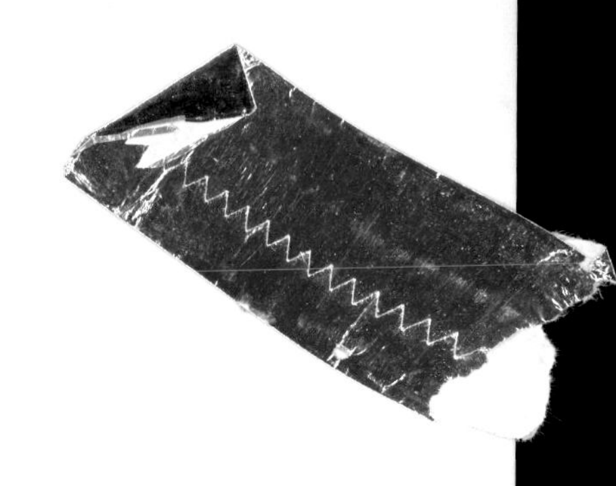

Chapter 5

# *HOLY GROUND*

*"Put off your shoes from your feet, for the place on which you are standing is holy ground."* Exodus 3:5

Thus Yahweh has visited Enochville. He did not come to destroy the city for its corruption and violence as in the days of the flood (Genesis 6:5-12), or to visit it with fire and brimstone as he did Sodom and Gomorrah (Genesis 18:20-21; 19:24-28). He did not come, as the Zealots hoped, with power and a host of angels to overthrow the glory of Rome and of every predatory nation and to give victory to the Jews in a holy war. Least of all did God come to be taken on a guided tour so as to be impressed by Enochville's glories.

He came secretly, without trumpets or halo or flash of visible glory, so that he might come in love and not wrath, to save and not to destroy. "For God sent the Son into the world, not to condemn the world, but that the world might be saved through him" (John 3:17). In the prologue of his Gospel, John describes the tender gentleness of the visit: "The true light that enlightens every man was coming into the world. He was in the world, and the world was made through him, yet the world knew him not. He came to his own home, and his own people received him not. But to all who received him, who believed in his name, he gave power to become children of God" (John 1:9-12). What a strange visit! What incredible love!

The visit was not in vain. Not only was Enochville granted a reprieve from the wrath that should have destroyed it; there was also salted in Cain's city a new citizenry, born of God, marked through baptism with the name of Jesus and the address of the new Jerusalem (Revelation 3:12; 7:3; 14:1; 22:14). Within Enochville, Yahweh founded "the city of the living God, the heavenly Jerusalem, the assembly of the first-born who are enrolled in heaven" (Hebrews 12:22-23). In this city, God's reconciled people are themselves the temple (John 2:17-22; 1 Corinthians 3:17; Ephesians 2:21-22). The quiet visitation of God goes on in them. As the living voice of God's word, they beseech Enochville on behalf of Christ to be reconciled to God (2 Corinthians 5:20). They have been given a place to stand, and from it they are to move the earth.

### Holy Ground and Naked Feet

The ground on which God's people stand before him is not the "cursed" ground of Cain, but "holy ground." Like Moses, they have "seen a great sight" (Exodus 3:3), a world aflame with God's wrath, and yet, like that "burning bush," not consumed! Out of that flame comes the voice of God saying, "Put off your shoes from your feet, for the place on which you are standing is holy ground" (Exodus 3:5). God has prepared this ground for them, but they must stand on it with naked feet. No comfortable, self-fabricated shoes dare insulate them from it. Only a barefooted church can live in reconciliation, and thus be the voice of God's reconciliation to Enochville.

This imagery of barefootedness, as against the self-protection implied by shoes, brings to focus the continuing danger of disguised alienations by which God's people in Old Testament and New so readily deceive themselves. A process of subtle insulating always seems to occur. The church celebrates and preserves the fulness of Yahweh's mercy and truth (Ephesians 3:19) by encasing it in forms of worship and of doctrine. Then it stands upon these forms as though the forms themselves are the "holy ground," not realizing that the forms have become "shoes." They get in the way of God's Word. They protect the wearer from what God is really saying! An associated imagery is that of emptiness. The forms are like wineskins. Once flexible and full of the wine of God's Spirit and truth, they tend to become hard and empty. They may still have the appearance and offer the promise of wine, but those who cherish and look to them are deceived (Matthew 9:17; John 2:3).

The people of God need and must have forms, to be sure, for it is by forms that they give expression to their great treasure. By forms and rhythms of worship, music, and hymnody, they remember and praise God for what he has done, is doing, and will do for them. Because they are a gathered people, they need a gathering place. They summon the skills of architects and artists and the craftsmanship of builders, together with their own willing offerings, to build houses of worship. Because they live in Enochville they adapt to their own use structures of authority and of discipline, and the advantages of efficient organization. They also formulate the truth of God into words of doctrine; they systematize it for the sake of efficiency in teaching, and for distinguishing divine truth from human distortion and error. They treasure the written Word of Holy Scripture, which preserves to them the voices of prophets and apostles who knew Yahweh and spoke by his Spirit. They learn the skills of interpreting the Scriptures as the living fountain for understanding and preaching the Word, and as a guard against alien spirits. All of this is both inevitable and necessary, for the church is in the world; its people are called to use the varied gifts God has invested in them, thus to fulfil the will of God as his servants.

The difficulty is that the forms always tend to attract attention to themselves, so that the content of God's truth, which they intended to celebrate, begins to evaporate. The forms are comprehensible to the people who created them. Even Enochville can comprehend and appreciate the cultural heritage of the church's forms. But the Spirit and the life of Yahweh is not comprehensible in that way. So the shoes begin to get in the way of the holy ground. The forms assert themselves as though they were the message. Knowledge of the forms parades itself as though it were the knowledge of Yahweh!

Every faithful worshiper realizes this to some degree. With body and voice he participates in the familiar forms, only to discover suddenly that his mind and heart have been occupied elsewhere. The artistry of organ and choir, the magnificent sound of singing, the eye-appeal of the churchly setting, may generate a thrill of cultural emotionalism that feels very religious, and yet convey nothing of the word of God. For God did not reveal himself to Cain through emotional awe, but by the word of the cross which kills in order to raise up to new life. Yahweh did not come to Enochville through rituals perfectly enacted in the temple, but through the unholy darkness and horror that surrounded Calvary. Our God is not sweetness and light, but a consuming fire (Hebrews 12:29). It is only by his grace that we are not utterly consumed.

The warning must ring very clear: "You shall not take the name of the Lord your God in vain!" (Exodus 20:7). You shall not treat the name of the Lord your God as though it were mere words, an idle and empty form! "For the Lord will not hold him guiltless who takes his name in vain," that is, he will not hold him as a member of his holy people. That is why the prophets out of their fulness are driven to expose and pronounce judgment upon Israel's proud reliance on the faithfulness of their worship and the purity of their performance, all of which has become so empty. "I will accept no bull from your house. . . If I were hungry I would not tell you. . . What right have you to recite my statutes, or take my covenant on your lips?" (Psalm 50:7-16). "Hear the word of the Lord, you rulers of Sodom! . . . What to me is the multitude of your sacrifices? Who requires of you this trampling in my courts?" (Isaiah 1:10-13). "I hate, I despise your feasts, and I take no delight in your solemn assemblies. Even though you offer me burnt offerings and cereal offerings, I will not accept them. . . Take away from me the noise of your songs; to the melody of your harps I will not listen" (Amos 5:21-23).

When Jesus spoke the word of God to Jerusalem, the problem he encountered was that of emptiness and insulating shoes—forms of ritual obedience without the knowledge of God. "You have made void (empty) the word of God by your tradition" (Matthew 15:6). You debate questions like paying tithes on garden vegetables, and "have neglected the weightier (the heavy-content) matters of the law, justice and mercy and faith" (Matthew 23:23). Jesus focused the problem by way of a parable—the unclean spirit driven out of a man returns, and finds the house "empty, swept, and put in order." Cleaned out, newly painted, but *empty!* The forms are there, but the content is lost. So the forms get filled, secretly and unknown, with an alien content. The same old spirit comes back sevenfold and makes his home within the very forms of true worship! "And the last state of that man becomes worse than the first" (Matthew 12:43-45). Israel has the appearance of the waiting bride and the form of the lamps, but "no oil" (Matthew 25:3), hence no light to dispel the midnight darkness. "I desire steadfast love and not sacrifice, the knowledge of God rather than burnt offerings," says the Lord. (Hosea 6:6; Matthew 9:13; 12:8) But what God gets is loyalty to forms, the pretense of a son who says, "I go, sir," but does not really know what it means to serve his father (Matthew 21:30).

"But Israel does not know, my people does not understand," Yahweh complains in his frustration (Isaiah 1:3). The people do battle to protect their forms against the word of the living God. Fullness is a threat to their dried wineskins, hence they reject it. The prophets who proclaim the riches of God's mercy and truth, and who demand the fruits of God's Spirit, are resisted, suppressed, and persecuted, all in the name of Yahweh (Matthew 21:34-39; 22:6; 23:38). Darkness resists and hates the light (John 1:5; 3:19-20; 9:39-41). "He who has ears, let him hear!" Jesus cries (Matthew 13:9). But the hearers are already full! Why should they listen?

Thus, subtle forms of insulation have become between, to prevent the feet of God's people from standing on the holy ground, and to keep the voice of the Lord from penetrating the hearers. The Pharisees cry, "Moses, Moses" (John 5:45-46; 9:28-29; Luke 16:29-31), just as the church cries, "The Bible, the Bible," yet does not know how to hear what the Lord is really saying. Pharisee and church alike may boast in the purity of a doctrinal system, yet without comprehending the wonder of their only true purity, bought through the blood of the cross and sealed to God's people in the washing of baptism (Ephesians 5:25-27; 1 John 1:7). Institutional advancement becomes the mark of status and worth in the church, just as it does in Enochville. The authority of high office, backed by popular confidence and symbolized by an inner sanctum lined with carpeting and drapes, readily displaces the authority inherent in the word of the cross. The smooth operation of the institution with maximal efficiency and minimal friction is mistaken for the unity and power of the church. Statistical progress becomes the mark of divine approval. Going to church, giving to the church, and doing church work constitute service and obedience to God. To bring more people in under the forms of the church is the church's mission. To censure firmly, and even exclude anyone who questions the validity of some theological tradition or ecclesiastical practice, constitutes "discipline." By such discipline, officially exercised, the church keeps its people from being troubled or misled, overcomes "offense," preserves "truth," creates "unity," and assures itself of "peace."

Meanwhile, the word of God with its devastating exposure of Enochville's sin and death does not break through at all. What Enochville sees instead is the smugness, judgmentalism, hypocrisy, division, and emptiness of the church as an institution. This is no problem for Enochville. That kind of church is readily absorbed into the rest of Enochville's alienations.

### Barefooted Listening

"Put off your shoes from your feet!" Listen now to what God is saying to you, person to person, as one whom he loves. Let nothing come between to distract you. When you stand before the burning fire of Yahweh's wrath and yet mercy, you are not impressive or important as Enochville measures such things. Your high office, responsibility, or self-estimation count for nothing in the sight of God. Neither are you inferior and worthless, for all your feelings of guilt and inadequacy and self-pity. You are simply a person whom God loves and wants, for whom Christ died. You are a small and hungry child, starving for the bread of life, thirsty for the living water, needing to taste God's new wine. God has something to say to you, like a voice from heaven. This is what he says:

"I am the Lord your God! You belong to me. I created you, and the world and the time into which I have set you. I have also delivered you from the wrath and judgment that should rightly condemn and destroy you. I did it for you in Jesus' death, the Jesus whose name you now share, because in your baptism I said to you as to him, 'You are my beloved son, with whom I am well pleased.' That word stands forever. Heaven and earth will pass away, but not that word of mine to you (Luke 21:33). Therefore, listen to no accuser who contradicts me! Judgment day is past and the accusation, however true and shameful, has no power over you. No one shall snatch you out of my hand (John 10:27-30). I have given you a dignity and a glory that transcends and puts to shame all human calculations of glory. Your glory is to be my son, my saint, my elect, my heir. Your glory is to know me, and to stand before me unashamed.

"So don't look at yourself any more, as though you could discover your personhood by introspection. Don't listen to voices any more—not the voice of conscience, not the voices of people who compliment you or criticize you, build you up or tear you down. Listen only to me! And if you want to *see* me, look for me at that one place where I have made myself visible so that you could see me. Look for me in that eternal cross-section of human history, where all humanity in despising my Son despised me, in conspiring against my Son conspired against me! And then see how he, for your sake and mine, bore away into his death the wrath that should have destroyed the world and you. Do you want to see my glory? See it there!"

That's what your God says to you from heaven, out of the *past,* as he tells you who you are! But he also tells you what you need to know about your *future*. Put off your shoes, therefore, and listen once again. This is what he says:

"Thus says the Lord, your God and your Father, don't be afraid of tomorrow, and don't grasp for it. I know where you are in space and in time. I have created and redeemed your life, and I continue to unfold it to you day by day. I promise that you will have daily bread, for I am your Father, and shall not make sport of you by giving you a stone for bread or a serpent for fish (Matthew 7:7-11). Ask me and I shall surely hear! I also promise to deliver you from evil. Don't be angry if I seem to treat you unequally. Don't be afraid if I lead you into the valley of the shadow, into depression and temptation, into risk of suffering and actual suffering. Don't panic and run, and don't think you must save yourself. 'Call on me in the day of trouble, I will deliver you, and you shall glorify me' (Psalm 50:15). Beyond all your immediate tomorrows, I am the God who has promised you a kingdom, and it is my good pleasure to give it to you (Luke 12:32). My first-born Son, your brother, has already entered it for you, as a pledge that you shall have it in full (John 14:1-4). Even death cannot thwart my promise, for you shall rise as he rose, your biography made complete and glorious in his, to share his triumph eternally."

That is God talking about tomorrow, and his word stands forever! Finally, the voice from heaven tells you what kind of person you are to be *today* as his child. Once again, put off your shoes and stand directly and barefoot on his holy ground. He says:

"I am the Lord, your God and Father. I am Jesus Christ your master and brother. I have poured out upon you my Spirit. Your glory is to serve and follow me—but not like that worthless servant who feared that I was ' a hard man,' using him to do my dirty work while I reaped the profit, and who therefore hid the opportunity I gave him in the ground (Matthew 25:24). No, you serve me because you are my son and heir, and because you know and trust and belong to me and share my character and mind. Everything I have is yours already. You don't have to calculate how to keep out of trouble, for I have promised to deliver you from evil. You don't have to grasp for what your eye sees to be good, for I have promised to give you good beyond your dreams. You have no need to create yourself or prove anything about yourself. So now you have nothing to live and work for, except to serve me.

"Just listen to me, know me, be like me, and serve me without fear. This is what I want you to do. I want you to love your brother, and let no barrier divide you from him. It doesn't matter whether I put you into the position of Cain or of Abel, whether I make you low or high in this world. Love your brother even when he seems to be your enemy, just as I loved you when you were my enemy. My will is not hard to find. You don't have to chase up into the heavens or across the sea to find it. It is as near to you as my commandments, so that you may do it, and in doing it be a light in the dark world of Cain, and an instrument of mine to bring Cain home to me."

Now this is the Gospel, and the whole Bible is full of it. The real joy of Bible study lies not in learning many separate and intriguing things, but in finding that Gospel everywhere, like the "active ingredient" the chemist learns to isolate, all of it focusing finally on the central event and person who is our life and glory, Jesus our Lord and brother. This is the bread we need to be fed on, and when we feed on it richly, we discover that fragments always overflow in abundance, to be gathered and handed on to others, so that "nothing may be lost" (John 6:12). This is our water of life, and when we drink it freely it becomes a well of water, multiplying itself within us, surging out of our mouths again so that others may drink of it through us (John 4:14; 7:37-38). This Gospel is our joy and life, our beauty and power, our unfailing *rock,* our shelter and fortress against every accusation and fear. It is the holy ground on which we dare to stand naked and barefoot in the sight of God. For by this word, his righteousness and mercy are our everlasting clothing, and the shame of the cross of Christ is our deliverance from shame.

But this Gospel is also "the way" in which the children of God walk. By it the commandments make new and living sense to our hearts. Christ's "Spirit of wisdom and understanding" (Isaiah 11:2) rests upon us also. Our "delight is in the law of the Lord" (Psalm 1:2). His precepts are an enlightening for our eyes, more desirable than gold, sweeter than honey (Psalm 19:7-10). We begin to appreciate the wonder of the summons to "love the Lord your God with all your heart," for when he fills our heart, soul, and might with his riches, there is no room left to love anything else (Deuteronomy 6:4). The companion commandment, "You shall love your neighbor as yourself" (Matthew 22:34-40; Leviticus 19:18), sets the very direction of a life freed from self and enabled to look outward toward people and the world. For this God is God alone! There is no other God who called Israel out of the house of bondage, and a lost humanity out of its blindness, wrath, emptiness, and death.

Therefore, we want no other God! "You shall have no other gods before me," says our God. You shall put nothing between me and you, to cover my face with imaginings of your own, lest you no longer hear me or know me as I really am. Therefore, make no image of me which would liken me to something I created. Do not project upon me what your mind thinks I ought to be like. For then you will lose me, and the consequences will be the visit of death not only on you, but on the generations of children after you whom you deceived and formed in your own image rather than in mine (Exodus 20:2-6).

"You shall not take the name of the Lord your God in vain." You shall not treat my name as though it were empty words, or set your heart on forms of religion which have become a hollow mockery of my name. For if you do, I shall not hold you guiltless. You will be the outsider, not my people. You will belong to Cain, utterly alienated, unable to know me, not wanting to know me. (Exodus 20:7)

"Remember the sabbath day to keep it holy. Six days you shall labor, and do all your work; but the seventh day is a sabbath to the Lord your God; in it you shall not do any work . . ." (Exodus 20: 8-11). For both your working and your resting come from me. Therefore seize the days I give you for work, seize the time and the energy, the imagination and the opportunity. Your work belongs to my work, and mine to yours. Your joy in your work belongs to my joy, even as the joy of my work is yours. But your work shall not become an obsession to you, as though you could create your own personhood by your labor and achievement or impress me with your successes. For if that is what work means to you, then the ground will again be cursed for you. The cursed ground will rise up against you to reveal that you are only dirt! You will fight it, but the ground will win! Therefore I teach you the rhythm of rest. Just as I command you to work, I also command you to rest and to enjoy rest. For the day may come when "rest" is all you have, when you cannot work because ability and opportunity and strength ceases. Therefore learn to rest, so that in resting you may remember and enjoy and praise me your Creator. You shall remember and notice how my good gifts are life to you, and how I called you out of Egypt to give you rest in the promised land (Deuteronomy 5: 15), and how I fulfilled your rest when I made everything new for you in the resurrection of Jesus Christ your Lord (Matthew 11:28-30; Hebrews 4:9-10; Revelation 14:13).

"Honor your father and your mother," for I did not create you to be a person alone, apart from other people (Exodus 20:12). That is why I made you through and within a family, so that you might discover and fulfil your personhood in relation to the people I gave to be yours, just as you are theirs. Therefore, honor your family as I have given you family. Belong to it fully, and do not despise it or cut yourself off from it, for that is lostness and death to you (Luke 15:24). You shall not despise and discard the society into which I have set you, neither shall you substitute for it a society of your own making, as though you were God and could "know good and evil" by your private eyesight. You shall honor your father and your mother by continuing to belong to them as one family, even as you grow to maturity. You shall not dishonor your home by indulging your sexuality secretly. You shall wait for the day when your father and your mother release you in the joy of the wedding. On that day you shall "leave" them for the sake of "cleaving" to one who is given you from another family, for the founding of a new home (Genesis 2:24; Matthew 19:3-6; Ephesians 5:31). On that day their parenthood toward you will not be dishonored or destroyed, but fulfilled.

But then, when I have made you a new society of husband and wife in one flesh, "You shall not commit adultery" (Exodus 20:14). You shall not trust your eyesight as it falls upon some man or woman other than the one I have given you (Matthew 5:28), but shall fulfil the call of love and unity toward your husband or wife alone, for you are one body in Christ. To love one another in marriage as one body is your first and most intimate obedience to my commandment to "love your neighbor as yourself" (Ephesians 5:33), as Christ loved you and gave himself for you (Ephesians 5:1-2, 25-30). This is what it means to know the Lord your God and to walk in his way, to be alienated no longer, but rather to be fellow citizens with the saints and of the family of God (Ephesians 2:19).

Thus, the relationship of children to parents, and of husband to wife in marriage, is the beginning of all personhood in society. From here you shall look out on the neighbors and strangers in the world beyond your home so as to love them as yourself (Leviticus 19:18, 34). They belong to you and you to them, side by side, neither over you nor under you. Therefore, you shall not establish or enlarge your own life at the cost of your neighbor's. You shall love him even if he does not love you, indeed, even if he acts as an enemy toward you, for that is how God in Christ loved you, his enemy (Romans 5:10; 12:20; Matthew 5:44-45). You shall not deal with your neighbor in violence, to kill him, when he is troublesome to you. You shall not try to be equal to him by stealing from him or destroying his property. What he has, I have given him, just as I have given you what I chose to give you. But if your enemy needs judgment and an avenger, you shall entrust the judgment to me (Romans 12:19; Deuteronomy 32:35) and to the powers I have ordained in Enochville to execute my wrath (Romans 13:4). Neither shall you make yourself judge over your neighbor by uttering your malice against him, or by putting him down by slander, or by taking advantage of him through treacherous and secret dealings. For he belongs to your own humanity, and in destroying him you destroy yourself (Exodus 20:13-16).

"You shall not covet" (Exodus 20:17). What I have given to your neighbor, I have withheld from you. You shall not even desire it. You shall not govern your actions by what your lustful eye tells you is "good" for you, or by what your fearful eye tells you is "evil." You shall fear me and love me, and trust in me above anything else. When you receive blessings, you shall give me thanks, when you experience troubles, you shall call upon me to deliver you (Psalm 50:15), for I am your life. Your glory is to know me and to "practice kindness, justice, and righteousness in the earth; for in these things I delight, says the Lord" (Jeremiah 9:23-24). You shall learn to be free and generous in giving, rather than lustful in getting, so that you may imitate my generosity toward you (Matthew 10:8; 2 Corinthians 8:9). For the rainfall of your generosity toward this dry earth is of a piece with mine, and the world shall know my mercy in yours (Matthew 5:16; Luke 6:36-38).

Thus the Lord God unfolds the life-style he has in mind for his people. It is called "the way of the Lord" (Isaiah 40:3), "the way of righteousness" (Matthew 21:32), "the holy way" (Isaiah 35:8), and the like. Those who know God and walk in that way are surrounded by promises. "Blessed is everyone who fears the Lord, who walks in his ways!" (Psalm 128:1) "The Lord knows the way of the righteous." (Psalm 1:6) "You shall not turn aside to the right hand or to the left. You shall walk in all the way which the Lord your God commanded you, that you may live, and that it may go well with you, and that you may live long in the land." (Deut. 5:32-35) "Because you have made the Lord your refuge . . . no evil shall befall you . . . For he will give his angels charge of you to guard you in all your ways . . . You will tread on the lion and the adder, the young lion and the serpent you will trample under foot . . . I will protect him, because he knows my name. When he calls to me, I will answer him; I will be with him in trouble . . . With long life I will satisfy him, and show him my salvation." (Psalm 91:9-16) "Behold, I have given you authority to tread upon serpents and scorpions, and over all the power of the enemy; and nothing shall hurt you." (Luke 10:19) "If you have faith and never doubt . . . even if you say to this mountain, 'Be taken up and cast into the sea,' it will be done." (Matthew 21:21)

What it means is that we walk God's straight path, trusting him in the face of every threat or obstacle, simply doing his will in everything we do. We will not crawl on our belly like the snake, eyes in the dirt, slithering to the right and to the left, governed by our limited vision of desire and fear. Isaiah 59:3-8 unfolds that deadly alternative with the climactic diagnosis, "They have made their roads crooked, no one who goes in them knows peace." "God made man upright," says the preacher (Ecclesiastes 7:29), and again "The wise man has his eyes in his head," a whole body length above the ground, so that he may see far and have his eye on God (Ecclesiastes 2:14).

To walk uprightly in the "paths of righteousness," fearing no evil, trusting the rod and staff of Yahweh, knowing his presence even when the way leads through "the valley of the shadow of death" (Psalm 23:3-4), that is the great adventure. It is both the definition of life, and its promise. It requires standing barefoot on the holy ground, and walking without sandals (Matthew 10:10) in the holy way.

### Testings

The temptations and the distractions are many, of course, and they never cease. The mind of Cain reasserts itself, seeking proofs, assembling statistics, forming God in its own image, charging that what cannot be seen or measured by man has no relevant existence. How do you know that "it shall go well with you?" What a fool you are! Admit it, there is nothing there!

The attack is directed against our sonship, for example, and the call to belong to God as his chosen people. By what right do those baptized into Christ claim to be so special? Surely God is not so provincial, so arbitrary, so unjust! What of all the other religions? Why should that one tiny event, the crucifixion of one Jew in a distant land over nineteen centuries ago take on such cosmic, universal significance? What arrogance, to claim that "God was in Christ, reconciling the world to himself" (2 Corinthians 5:19)! And indeed, it does seem foolish. Yet this is the very "folly" by which God is determined to "destroy the wisdom of the wise" (1 Corinthians 1:18-31).

Equally offensive are the promises of the kingdom of God. For who can believe seriously that the kingdom of God actually arrived in Jesus' death and resurrection, or that we live in that kingdom now under Jesus who received it in full and who reigns at the right hand of God? Who can believe that the kingdom is still coming, when those who bear his name will share fully his resurrection and glory. "What nonsense!" says the mind of Cain. "Who can believe seriously in the resurrection of the body from the grave?" There is no use arguing the case by rationality against rationality, of course. It remains the Father's business, what the ultimate kingdom and resurrection will look like (1 Corinthians 15:35-38) or when it will come (Acts 1:7). But the holy ground does not tremble. The promises stand sure, made visible for us in Christ and his resurrection. By his word of promise, God frees his people from the need to pursue a future and kingdom of their own devising, as well as from the need to flee in terror from death and the threats that each tomorrow may raise against them. The promises of God make possible a life of hope, and therefore of love and of sacrifice. The hope they offer is infinitely more sure than all the fragile optimism of desire and fear by which blind Enochville encourages itself!

Then there are all the temptations which proceed from our eyesight and judgment in knowing good and evil. What good is it to honor parents and other authorities, if those who exercise authority are obviously perverse, selfish, tyrannical, and even stupid? Why should sex be reserved for marriage, and its passions restrained by questionable inhibitions and outmoded traditions? Why should property be respected, especially if its rich corporate owners are the oppressors of the poor? Why should anyone be denied the freedom to do what seems right in his own eyes (Judges 21:25)?

Or again, what good is it to be named sons of God when God treats his sons unequally as in the case of Cain, or when he answers your need for bread by giving you stones (Matthew 7:9; 4:2-3)? What good is it to live quietly in hope of the kingdom and to endure oppressions without complaint, when the oppressors take advantage of you, and the kingdom does not come, and there is absolutely no sign that it ever will come? What good is it to serve God only, when the service he demands calls for you to love those who take advantage of you, and to walk into death and the cross with no angels in sight to deliver you?

What of all the injustices? Why should not that elder son, who worked so faithfully for so many years, be indignant and angry when his renegade younger brother gets welcomed with a big party? When did the Father ever give thought to throwing such a party in appreciation for *him*? (Luke 15:28-30) Doesn't the elder brother have a point? And doesn't Cain have a point in his anger against Abel, the visible symbol of the inequity and oppression under which Cain suffers? And how can anybody *not* feel high when he is being recognized and complimented, and down when he is ignored or accused—in spite of anything the word of God says? Isn't it a pretentious waste of time and effort, as well as a psychological impossibility, to love somebody who is hurting you? Who can be expected to understand the abstruse systems of doctrine, so unrelated to life, which the church imposes on its members in the name of orthodoxy? Who can trust any of the conflicting interpretations given to the Bible with all its history-conditioned humanness, or expect seriously to hear in it God's own "voice from heaven"?

The weapons of Satan's testing (Matthew 4:1, 10) are many, and no child of God escapes the battle. They strike me down most furiously in the early morning. It is still dark. I toss in bed, having awakened too soon. Then all my stupidities and uncertainties, my inadequacies and unanswered questions, my guilt and my failures of energy and of courage—all rise together in unholy laughter to mock me, as though to say, "This ground you profess to stand on, it's all words, futile and empty words! The only reason you still cling to those words is because you have gone too far to let them go!" I am in utter darkness then, able to see nothing of what I want to see, for what I want to see is some evidence of God! I understand the Psalmist who confesses, "I flood my bed with tears" (Psalm 6:6), and who speaks of the night as a time of weeping (Psalm 30:5).

Moses must have been caught in that kind of depression when he cried to the Lord, "Show me thy glory!" (Exodus 33:18-23) The Lord answered the prayer in a strange way. He put Moses into the cleft of a rock while he passed by, and held his hand over him so that Moses was in utter darkness. But then the Lord withdrew his hand, so that Moses could see him from behind, after he had passed by. Thus in the dark hour of my testing I am covered by the Lord's own hand. But when the morning comes I see him again, though from behind. I see the cross, and on it the Son of God who loved me and gave himself for me, and my baptism by which God wrote his own name on my forehead in his own script (Revelation 7:3; 14:1). And that is enough. I am back on holy ground, barefoot. That ground is my everlasting rock.

**Knowing God**

Thus the children of God, in the "spirit of sonship" (Romans 8:14-17), see God and know him. They know him through the word of the Gospel of Christ, which came to them "in power and in the Holy Spirit and with full conviction" (1 Thessalonians 1:5). They see him by looking to Christ and to the mercy revealed in his death and resurrection, for in seeing him they see the Father (John 14:8-11). Their will is to follow Jesus in doing the Father's will, without reservation or private agenda (John 7:17). They are "the pure in heart" who "see God" (Matthew 5:8). They see his face shining on them in tender and patient pleasure, his mouth turned upward in a smile of blessing (Numbers 6:24-26; Psalm 4:6; 67:1). If their own hearts rise up still to accuse and condemn them, they know that God is greater than their hearts; he knows it all and yet does not condemn (1 John 3:20). For "there is now no condemnation for those who are in Christ Jesus" (Romans 8:1), and no accuser (Romans 8:33).

The people of God look at the world around them and know that it, too, remains God's. They see Cain's city and know how God sees it, how he loves and rules it, even though he remains hidden to it, and how he protects it by his own mark from and against itself. And they know people, with a peculiar and unique knowledge. It is something like the knowledge described in Genesis 2:25, "the man and his wife were both naked, and were not ashamed." The saints of God have been discovered in their own nakedness, but the love of God in Christ has so covered them that they are not ashamed. They understand, therefore, what the nakedness is which Enochville is compelled to conceal by its many fig-leaf devices. Their knowledge of people does not have to be developed by long conversations, vast accumulations of information, or sensitivity encounters. It is the kind of understanding Jesus had, of whom John 2:25 reports that he "knew all men, and needed no one to bear witness of man; for he himself knew what was in man." Such knowledge of people, in love, becomes possible when the fences of alienation have been broken down. God's reconciled saints understand what alienation is, how it works, and how it traps people in a prison of "sin" which they themselves cannot comprehend. They know the pressures of desire and fear, the exhilaration of success and the despondency that comes with defeat and evidence of worthlessness. Because the saints know how the knowledge of good and evil works in themselves, they can understand how it works itself out in the aggressions and defenses of Enochville. They understand, but they are not dismayed. The barriers still exist, but they have no power to kill Christ again, or to smother the love of God that broke through into the world through him, or to quench the word and Spirit of his life.

The saints stand and walk on holy ground. They find life in the mercy of God. They receive all God gives them with thanksgiving, and they trust him to deliver them whenever they experience hardship and trouble. They serve God where they are. Their work is of a piece with God's work, and their joy in it is God's joy. They are willing for God to distribute both gifts and sufferings unequally, as he pleases, to "be gracious to whom he will be gracious" and "show mercy on whom he will show mercy" (Exodus 33:19). They harbor no sense of inferiority or envy toward those who seem to be higher in the eyes of Enochville, nor do they feel superior or condescending toward those whom Cain's city judges to be low and unimportant. Neither irritations and frustrations, nor deliberate and obvious sins, will drive them to self-pity and anger. For the enemy is not people. The enemy is "sin couching at the door," ready to deceive and destroy. The enemy is ignorance of God, obsession with the arrogant and seductive wisdom of knowing good and evil, and all the subsequent alienations by which people are driven to respond and act as they do. But if sin raises barriers, those who live under the mercy of their heavenly Father treat such barriers with patient courage and humor, refusing to perpetuate or even to acknowledge them.

This is the character of "the city of the living God" planted within the city of Cain (Hebrews 12:22). It fills the world and life with new possibilities!

## Chapter 6

# *HOLY WAR*

> *For though we live in the world we are not carrying on a worldly war, for the weapons of our warfare are not worldly but have divine power to destroy strongholds. We destroy arguments and every proud obstacle to the knowledge of God, and take every thought captive to obey Christ.* 2 Corinthians 10:3-5

The task of the church is to subvert Enochville from within, destroy its strongholds, break down its walls, and take the citizenry of Cain captive for and in the name of Jesus Christ. But it is a strange warfare. Its intention is not to hurt but to heal, not to suppress but to free, not to degrade but to honor. It is a tender warfare of gentle subversion, uncompromising to be sure, and yet full of love and hope and peace even in the fighting. The enemy is not people but alienation. The attackers would rather be wounded than wound, serve than be served. Their goal and fervent prayer is to find Cain the fugitive, set his feet again on God's holy ground, and bring him home.

St. Paul's battle plan, quoted above, is simple and yet comprehensive. We begin with his first proposition.

**"We live in the world"**

Though Canaan had been promised him as a possession, Abraham lived there "as in a foreign land" (Hebrews 11:9). He was satisfied to be the stranger, and made no attempt to "take over" what God was not ready to entrust to him in any political way.

The situation of the church is similar. "All things are yours," St. Paul tells the Corinthians, "whether . . . the world or life or death or the future, all are yours; and you are Christ's; and Christ is God's." (1 Corinthians 4:21-23) Christians who live by such a promise have no need to covet the world. They know that ownership is finally not a matter of Enochville's titles and deeds, but of the God whose children and heirs they are.

In Enochville Christians are content to be the alien minority. They do not attempt to seize or disrupt Enochville or to impose on Cain's city ideals and strategies which it is incapable of comprehending. They respect and participate in its arts and games, its economy and government, its creativity and technology. They understand how their God in his hidden way governs the city for its good. They make themselves at home, just as Jeremiah advised Judah's exiles to make themselves at home in Babylon: "Build houses . . . plant gardens . . . multiply there . . . But seek the welfare of the city where I have sent you into exile, and pray to the Lord on its behalf, for in its welfare you will find your welfare." (Jeremiah 29:4-7) Christians enjoy the blessings which their God continues to shower even upon the city of Cain (Matthew 5:45). At the same time they share willingly in whatever judgments God inflicts upon it: pestilence, crime, war, and other disasters.

As they take part in the government and economy of Enochville, Christians do not pretend to some higher wisdom which enables them to dispense with eyesight, judgment, and common sense. They calculate strategies just as Enochville does, by setting advantage against disadvantage, and choosing that action which seems to offer the best hope for good with the least new burden of evil. Because their ultimate confidence rests not in their wisdom but in the care and promises of their God, they enjoy a remarkable freedom to subordinate an immediate personal advantage to the larger and longer range advantage of city and land. They can put their neighbor into the center of calculation, love him as themselves, and thus risk personal loss. Even here, however, they are employing the kind of wisdom Enochville is able to comprehend. They negotiate in terms of Enochville's laws, use Enochville's money, talk Enochville's language.

Because they understand so well that Enochville *must* operate by the wisdom of human eyesight and calculation, Christians are in a position to make valuable contributions to its government. For example, without demanding a love of which Cain's city is incapable, they may sometimes persuade Enochville to endure an immediate "evil" out of sheer self-interest, in the prospect of a much greater though longer-range "good." Or again, Christians may recognize a need for legislation which might seem to compromise a moral principle (like regulating divorces), if that will help Enochville's governors maintain at least some measure of control. For government as such must not be allowed to fall into ridicule and disrepute through the actions of those who defy unenforceable laws with impunity.

Christian citizens will insist that Enochville not evade the necessity of thinking, for it is by thinking that Cain's city pursues the good and avoids the evil. Christians help Enochville think, and seek no shortcuts. They are different, not in their thought processes, but only in their awareness of the limitations of human calculation. They know the divine irony that the best wisdom readily and unpredictably backfires, that the ground planted in hope and at great effort may yet yield "thorns and thistles" (Genesis 3:18). Therefore, these aliens in Enochville offer the city of Cain one more benefit. They "pray to the Lord on its behalf" (Jeremiah 29:7). For ultimately, the welfare of Enochville does not depend on the wisdom of its devices, but on the continued mercy of the hidden God. It is God alone who makes the wisdom of man good and preserves the wise as well as fools from their folly.

Enochville, therefore, has no occasion to become irritated at the church, or to regard the church as subversive, disruptive, or incomprehensibly interfering with its political processes. Submission to and participation in the structure of Enochville belongs to the strategy of the saints, a strategy which also prevents them from attaching the name of Christ to false battles on false fronts. That is St. Peter's point (1 Peter 2:11-13) when he pleads with Christians as "aliens and exiles" to "maintain good conduct among the Gentiles," and to disarm any suspicion of political subversion or threat. "Be subject," he says, "for the Lord's sake to every human institution."

**"The weapons of our warfare are not worldly"**

St. Paul defines the "stronghold" of Enochville when he adds, "We destroy arguments and every proud obstacle to the knowledge of God" (2 Corinthians 10:3-5). Cain's proud obstacle to the knowledge of God is his determination to trust his opened eyes, and thus to be "wise" and "like God" in "knowing good and evil" (Genesis 3:5-6). That stronghold must come down if Enochville's alienations are to be overcome, if the city of Cain is to hear and know God again.

The strongholds to be overthrown in Enochville are not its structures of government, or police, or army, or industry, or technology, or economics. These are indeed visible symbols of power, and their power is dramatically real. Such power may also be abused and become the instrument of suppression and injustice, deliberately or unconsciously, against individuals or minority groups. Yet Enochville's structures belong to its necessary essence. If they reveal alienation, they also represent and contain Enochville's adjustment and accommodation to alienation. They are the ground upon which Enochville as a city of alienated humanity can even exist. They are a gracious gift of the hidden God.

Therefore, the church cannot bring in the kingdom of God and save the world by simply taking over Enochville's structures and putting its own people in charge with their supposedly higher moral insight and inspiration. That was the medieval theory of the two swords in the hand of the Pope. It didn't work then and it never will. The church can fall into such an illusion only when it has become a structure itself, pitting its own structure against Enochville's, on the assumption that if a structure bears the name "church," it must somehow be "holier" and closer to God than structures which belong to the "world," or that the church by its structure can exert a pious influence on the world. For even the structure of the organized church is the product of the wisdom of man. Surely the church will have some structure. But if the church begins to act as though its *power* lay in pressures it can exert through its organization, it has succumbed to Enochville and will be nothing more than another Enochville structure, even if it wins.

Such noble values as peace, prosperity, dignity, liberty, and equal justice for all are no peculiar province of the church, after all. Enochville itself knows about them, and accords them a very high honor as a matter of moral principle! The difficulty in Enochville lies in fixing the *cause* of the obvious conflicts that keep arising —poverty, repression, injustice, crime, and war—and then arriving at some strategy of cure. Some of its citizens may feel that the root cause of all Enochville's oppressions is its capitalistic economy. Others argue vehemently that this very economy, offering the hope of gain as an incentive to work, and subject to conflicting pressures out of the special interests of management and labor, has produced the broadest freedom and prosperity the world has known. Again, some in Enochville see "law and order," enforced by police, courts, jails, and armies, as the very instrument of oppression, while others see it as the bastion of stability and freedom in the face of growing violence and disrespect for law. Everything depends, however, on what people *see* with their opened eyes, and on the judgments they form as they try to be "wise" in their "knowledge of good and evil."

Christians have no special divine wisdom in such matters. They, too, depend on eyesight and common sense. Some may ally themselves as citizens with the forces of protest in Enochville, while others will sympathize in the name of realism with the struggles and imperfections of the existing authority. Both are acting, and must act, on the limited wisdom of what they can see, and on how they interpret the evidence. In the face of what can become a very powerful political disagreement among them, Christians will be united at least in this, that they count finally, not on their own wisdom, but on the mercy of God to bring blessing out of their actions, and to deliver Enochville from the potentially disastrous consequences of the hidden follies into which it falls as it tries so hard to be wise.

Christians of every political persuasion will understand this, too, that political actions serve at best only to achieve a more effective accommodation to alienation in Enochville. They do not get at

Enochville's stronghold. They do not effect reconciliation. Beyond all political efforts to implement a more just and free society, there lies the ultimate "revolution" rooted in the cross. What the Christian is really after is a "new creation," in which Enochville ceases to be Enochville and becomes instead, "the city of the living God." What he is really praying for is to bring Cain home.

**The weapons of our warfare . . . have divine power to destroy strongholds.**

David could not fight Goliath in Saul's armor (1 Samuel 17:39). Neither can the church get at the strongholds of Enochville if it fights with Enochville's tactics and weaponry.

For the enemy is not physical fortresses and not people. "We are not contending against flesh and blood," St. Paul reminds us (Ephesians 6:12). The enemy is "the prince of the power of the air, the spirit that is now at work in the sons of disobedience," who causes men to live "in the passions of [their] flesh, following the desires of body and mind" so that they are "by nature children of wrath" (Ephesians 2:2-3). That is Paul's way of describing our imprisonment under the wisdom of "knowing good and evil." Elsewhere he calls the enemy "sin." "Let not sin reign in your mortal bodies, to make you obey their passions. Do not yield your members to sin as instruments of wickedness." (Romans 6:12-13) "You were slaves to sin," he says, and "the wages of sin is death" (Romans 6:20, 23). Cain's enemy, too, was not Abel, or circumstances, or the injustice of Yahweh, but "sin" couching at the door and desiring to have him (Genesis 4:7).

Jesus knew that enemy well. He fought "sin" in Gethsemane, not with a sword, but with the word of God, prayer, and bloody sweat.

"What?" said sin to Jesus, "Does your God, who called you his beloved Son, agree with Caiaphas that 'one man should die for the people', and that it should be *you*? What kind of God is he if he imposes that on you, after all you have already done for him? Don't fall for it, Jesus! It's all a trick, a lie! There isn't going to be any kingdom, any resurrection! Open your eyes, quit playing the fool! Shake off the dust of your feet against Jerusalem! Call God's bluff! If God destroys the city because there are no righteous in it, as he destroyed Sodom and Gomorrah, let him! What more can you be expected to do? But if he doesn't destroy it, then you will know once and for all that God is dead, an illusion and a lie, and that people have nothing to live for except their own thoughts, desires, and fears. Don't be stupid, Jesus! There is no city of the living God. There is only Enochville!"

If that is not enough, Satan and sin will say, "See that cross? Do you know what it is to be crucified, and to die? If you walk out that gate and let them arrest you, it will be like leaping off the pinnacle of the temple, with the hard pavement a hundred and fifty feet below! Look down! Do you see it? For all God's promises of care and protection, there will be no angels, no miracle to save you, and no turning back! A smashed body, a horrible death—is that what you want? Can you possibly believe that's what the God you call your Father wants?" (See Matthew 4:5-7.)

Eyesight and the wisdom of man against the word of God, that is the battle of all battles! Jesus clung to the word. By that word he laid down his life for the sheep whom he loved (John 10:11). It was not a waste. God raised him from the dead as he had promised and as the Scriptures also had said (Hosea 6:2). The day of wrath was past, borne away in the blood of the lamb. "It is done" (Revelation 21:6). The holy city, the new Jerusalem, has come.

The word of God became visible in the flesh as Jesus stood alive before his disciples on Easter night. This word, filled with the Spirit Jesus breathed upon them, turned their darkness into light. The horror of Calvary became God's gift of love, offered to the disciples and the world as their own possession. By Jesus' word they had forgiveness, peace, joy, vision, hope, freedom, and courage. Every treasure of Christ became theirs. They saw the world as Jesus had seen it, and knew the Father as Jesus knew him. This word raised them from death to life, and when it then poured out of their lips in testimony to others, it was the very power of God for salvation to everyone who believed it (Romans 1:16). The word of God is "the sword of the Spirit," the mighty weapon of the church's assault upon the strongholds of Enochville (Ephesians 6:17).

Like a "voice crying in the wilderness" (Isaiah 40:3-5), the word of God lifts every valley and lowers every mountain. "Valley" stands for the depressed and defeated, against whom the evidences of suffering, disability, guilt, contempt and indifference of men, conspire to declare them worthless. The word of God refutes such evidences. It exalts the despairing by conferring on them freely the name and dignity of the saints and heirs of God. "Mountain" stands for the proud and satisfied who find in their achievements and in the admiration of men a proof of their superior worth. The word of God exposes the folly of their arrogant inferences and calls such sinners down from their illusory mountain, before the wrath of God and the laughter of the dust destroys them. For the worth of a man lies in the mercy of God alone, and in the sonship that he must receive *freely* or not at all. Thus, when the word of God has lifted up a Cain from the valley of his depression, despair, and anger, when it has brought down a fallen Abel from the mountain of his self-satisfaction and condescending superiority, then the weapon of the church's warfare has demonstrated its "divine power to destroy strongholds" (2 Corinthians 10:4).

The power to raise valleys and lower mountains, that is what Jesus means when he commissions his disciples to "forgive" sins or "retain" them (John 20:23), to "bind" people or to set them free (Matthew 16:19; 18:18). All the authority of heaven is invested in the words men speak on earth (Matthew 9:9). The treasure of God's mercy and truth is invested in "earthen vessels," that is, in human preachers who in their own persons have no authority at all. Yet the message itself is filled with all the authority of God!

Therefore, the church has no reason to despair of its words, as though they were somehow futile and empty, like the "noisy gong" or "clanging cymbal" or "indistinct bugle" of which St. Paul speaks (1 Corinthians 13:1; 14:7-8).

The word of reconciliation is filled with the *history* of an actual event, the death and resurrection of Jesus Christ, in whom God has invested himself and his total mercy for our life and hope. By the proclamation of Christ, God attaches that event to the concrete and personal life-history of the hearer, so that in him who was made sin for us, we might become the righteousness of God (2 Corinthians 5:21). The word is as real as that history is real!

Furthermore, the word of God does not deteriorate into trite aphorisms, empty cliches, tired doctrinal slogans. It is loaded with *thought,* not only God's thought but the continual hard thinking of every saint who speaks that word. "We take every thought captive to obey Christ," St. Paul says (2 Corinthians 10:5). Paul, like the old prophets and like Jesus himself, was a thinker. His letters show how he analyzed the "proud obstacles" which the natural heart of man continually raises against the word and knowledge of God. Paul searched and thought about the Scriptures and their meaning, about the cross and what God was saying to the world by it, about people and their defenses, about sin and its persuasive tyranny in the knowledge of good and evil, about how to penetrate the wall so as to make Enochville see the wisdom of God hidden in the foolishness of the cross. And so the church today is challenged to think, so as to "destroy arguments and every proud obstacle to the knowledge of God."

Such thinking depends on *love,* and cannot happen without love. Only love generates the energy and desire to think, and meanwhile to "bear all things, believe all things, hope all things, endure all things" (1 Corinthians 13:7). It was love that sent Jesus to Galilee to gather the lost with the cry, "Repent, for the kingdom of heaven is at hand," and then to hardened Jerusalem, and even to the cross. It was love that kept St. Paul going on his mission to gather the Gentiles, even in the face of persecution, prisons, lashings, and the threat of death. That kind of love is beyond the vision and capacity of Enochville. Its power lies not in attraction, or sympathy, or conscience, but in him who "first loved us" (1 John 4:19).

So love is not something the church *adds* to its words, as though involvement in mitigating a host of human sufferings were a way to make the "religious" message credible. The words themselves are filled with love. Love wants to say what is real, to penetrate the heart's defenses, to break through secret illusions, to feed Cain's hunger for worth and freedom and meaning with the only food that can really satisfy, to bring life where there is only death. This is what love wants to do, even while that same love searches how to fill those obvious and external hungers which Enochville can also see. But if the church does not love, the cure does not lie in weapons of accusation and proddings of conscience. Every failure of love testifies rather to some "proud obstacle to the knowledge of God" still to be searched out and diagnosed within Christians themselves, and which only the word of mercy and peace out of the cross has any power to penetrate and to heal.

The word of God is not empty, therefore. It is filled with the person of Jesus and his history, with thought and with love. Finally and climactically, it is filled with the *Spirit,* the Breath of the living God. St. Paul pictures it in 1 Corinthians 2:11-14. When God inhales, his Spirit knows his deepest, inmost thoughts. When God exhales, and in exhaling speaks words, his Spirit rides those words into our ears and thus into our own breathing, so that we comprehend what God is telling us, not merely on the level of intellect, but in our inmost personhood. Thus, through the wisdom that looks like foolishness, God evicts the wisdom of eyesight from its throne of tyranny over us.

But now, St. Paul confesses, that same Spirit of God harnesses our own minds and energies to Christ, and generates out of us the word that is meant for the next hearer. That is the secret dynamic of the Spirit. In all our hard thinking, captive as it is to Christ, the Spirit of Christ is at work. When the words are given us to speak, however fumbling and awkward they may seem to us, the Spirit of God has generated them and the Breath of God is riding on them. Therefore, when a stronghold in Enochville falls, it is not our wisdom and thinking that has done it, but the Spirit! For it is by foolishness that God has chosen to overthrow wisdom. By despised words that to eyesight are nothing, God has chosen to reduce to nothing what eyesight values as great and strong, "so that no human being might boast in the presence of God" (1 Corinthians 1:26-29).

That is the miracle of the Spirit of Christ! To believe in Christ is simply to have been overwhelmed and transformed by that miracle. This is the Spirit who pours out his gifts abundantly, in great variety, upon the saints whom he has gathered in Christ as one body (1 Corinthians 12:4-13; Ephesians 4:1-16). But all the gifts, distributed "by one and the same Spirit . . . as he wills" (1 Corinthians 12:11), have their focus and power in and from the word of the cross, that "sword of the Spirit" (Ephesians 6:17), "living and active, sharper than any two-edged sword, piercing to the division of soul and spirit," down into the most secret heart (Hebrews 4:12). The Spirit of Christ, alive and active in us and through the words we speak, is our secret weapon, and the only weapon to de stroy Enochville's strongholds and to bring Cain home.

**Church and Churches in Enochville**

"We live in the world . . . carrying on . . . our warfare," says St. Paul. Enochville sees that "we" in the form of churches, and what Enochville sees is not visibly ideal. Christians themselves, though breathing the Spirit of Christ, still bear within them the character of Cain's city. They fall readily into the pattern of trusting their sight, forgetting or not comprehending the wonder of what God has said to them. The impulses of desire and of fear exert great power still in determining their actions. In the joy of success and the dismay of failure, God's people easily lose sight of their real freedom, and imagine they must somehow still prove their worth to the world and to God. They are insulated from the holy ground then, yet without really knowing it.

As a result, the body of Christ finds itself splintering into factions, members at war with one another, or retreating for safety to a peace that resolves nothing and is no peace. The church becomes self-conscious. It feels itself accused and judged. It reacts defensively, as though it must justify its existence under Enochville's eyes of law. Enochville, in turn, measures the church by its institutional effectiveness, consigns it to the category of "religion," and pays it the painful homage of benign indifference. It appears that Enochville's stronghold is not only impregnable, but capable of devastating counterattack.

The Lord God ought to judge the church and give up on her, but he does not. Jesus continues to intercede for her (Hebrews 7:25; Romans 8:34; Isaiah 53:12) with the blood "that speaks more graciously than the blood of Abel" (Hebrews 12:24). For "Christ loved the church and gave himself up for her." He presents her to himself always as his bride on the day of the wedding, "without spot or wrinkle . . . holy and without blemish" (Ephesians 5: 25-27). When Satan like a prosecuting attorney stands before God to accuse the church of its shame and failure, God rebukes him! And the church, the gathered people of God, like a brand rescued from the fire, is clothed again in the beauty of God's forgiveness and righteousness (Zechariah 3:1-5). Somehow God is not insisting on an ideal church. He chooses the one that exists, which he holds as his own through baptism's unfailing word of promise, and which for all her self-contradictions continues to eat and drink the body and blood of Calvary's gory sacrifice for the forgiveness of her sins.

It is the word of God that creates the church, after all, and not external appearance of success or failure. That is why Christians gather regularly in worship around God's word, so that God may continue to speak to them in preaching and in the sacraments, bind them to himself and to one another, renew them in the Spirit of his peace and power, and then sprinkle them back into Enochville with his blessing upon them. The saints rejoice to hear God, and they respond in praise. For there is no higher honor they can give God for all his benefits than simply to receive and live on his gifts, or as Psalm 116:13 has it, to "take the cup of salvation and call upon the name of the Lord."

The worshiping community is a body of flesh and blood people made one in Christ. That is why they express their fellowship by gathering and organizing as a congregation, just as congregations then form larger church bodies. By way of such structuring of themselves, a congregation of Christians can consciously harness special gifts which God has invested in individual members for the common good. According to God's own will for them, they provide a ministry to preach and teach the word, administer the sacraments, lead them in worship and prayer, and speak God's blessing upon them (Ephesians 5:18-20; Numbers 6:22-27). They arrange to care for members who bear special burdens of temptation or suffering (Galatians 6:1-2). They join with parents in the task of bringing up children in the nurture of the Lord (Ephesians 6:4). They seek ways and encourage one another to share the word of reconciliation boldly in Enochville (Acts 4:29-31). They see needs as opportunities to love and serve those who are oppressed or suffer loss, also in the community beyond the congregation (Galatians 6:10). They pray for Enochville, and search for wisdom by which they themselves individually, and perhaps even as institution, may contribute positively in Enochville's struggle for a more just society against its forces of alienation (1 Peter 2:13-17).

The institutionalizing of the church brings with it a host of hazards as we have seen, above all, that the forms become "religion" in their own right, and emptied of their vital content and Spirit.

Christians will understand and treasure Yahweh's warning against taking his name "in vain." The church as organization is not equivalent to the organism which Christ calls his "body." It is not in itself the "holy ground" on which the saints stand. Nevertheless, the institutionalizing of the church is not in itself a perversion, neither would the church make itself more "holy" or "spiritual" or safe by dispensing with it. Anti-institutional criticisms have a valid point to make, but if the cure is to become simply un-institutional, then the walls of alienation have only taken another form. Privacy prevails over community, judgment over patient mercy, withdrawal over commitment. The institutionalizing of a community of saints has at least one great and inescapable benefit—a membership roster of particular flesh and blood people who have not chosen one another, but have been given to one another by Christ himself. To these people comes the challenge to make their fellowship in Christ work, to care for one another in love, and to maintain the unity of the Spirit in the bond of peace (Ephesians 4:1-3).

It is all too easy to stand on the outside like a judge, decrying a field for the weeds that have grown up among the wheat (Matthew 13:24-30), wanting nothing to do with what smacks of contradiction and hypocrisy. The harder task, and the call for love, is to belong to that field anyway, understanding how the "weed" character works also in oneself, dealing tenderly with what may not be weed at all but rather "a bruised reed" not to be broken (Matthew 12:20; Isaiah 42:3). The enemy, after all, is not people or institutions, but Satan who keeps sowing his own false seed. The power and hope of cure lies solely in Christ's "good seed," that is, in the sword of the Spirit, the word of God. The great need is to know that word, and how to both hear and speak it. Not the field but the good seed is what creates, defines, and preserves the church.

Thus, Christians in churches will do their institutional work boldly, confident of the Lord's blessing. There is great need and opportunity for "church work," meaning the portion of time and energy Christians invest in the work of their parish. The budget needs of the parish, and programs of education, service, and mission beyond the parish, are a valid opportunity for the exercise of love in generosity of giving, as the saints learn to imitate the free givingness of their God. Yet the rest of life is not thereby outside the church. Institutionalized church work is only one frontier of a total calling. The Christian is the son and servant of the Lord in everything he does, randomly or routinely, in his home or work or community, in his sleeping and waking, in times of pleasure as well as of pain. His whole life becomes one "living sacrifice, holy and acceptable to God" (Romans 12:1). This is his freedom, his fulfilment, his joy.

Much of this life is spent on the frontier of Enochville. By God's own design, the Christian finds himself thoroughly involved in the economy, politics, and culture of Enochville. By his own natural wisdom, he is able to understand the impulses that drive and control Cain's city. He does not have to look very hard to find the front line of reconciliation's holy warfare. He is on it day after day as he belongs willingly to Enochville's humanity, and works shoulder to shoulder with it toward achieving the greatest possible "good" and toward avoiding and overcoming "evil."

When it comes to pleading for Cain to come home, however, the Christian knows what it means to be a stranger in a strange land. Enochville is capable of no understanding, offers no alliance and no sympathy. That is why the call to "witness" for Christ seems so difficult, even impossible, to so many. Witnessing can happen only out of fulness, and the summons to be a voice for the word of God has a way of exposing emptiness. The saint of God knows that he ought to speak, but the words strike him now as mere cliche. He himself hardly understands their reality. How can he, then, speak and expect someone else to believe? He hears the counter-arguments of Enochville within himself, and has no real answer. What will he do if he hears them from someone to whom he tries to "witness"? Therefore, the call to speak in Jesus' name goes unanswered. Every other task of the church now looks simple by comparison. "Church work" of all kinds can be done in the relative security of sympathetic fellow-saints. Skill in fixing things is easily offered. Even sacrificial giving, which once seemed so impossible, turns out to be quite manageable. Once the decision is made, it becomes routine; the personhood of the giver can hide safely behind gifts which send others to the frontier.

But to take the sword of the Spirit, and by the word of God to expose Enochville's alienations so as to offer Christ's reconciliation, that requires fulness. And fulness cannot be demanded. It comes as the saints recognize the problem of their emptiness together, search the word together, and build one another up through the sharing of their gifts in love. It comes by prayer, and by willingness to bring their poverty to God, without putting on a pretense of understanding what they do not really understand at all. The Lord Jesus invites that kind of praying. "Ask, and it will be given you; seek, and you will find; knock, and it will be opened to you," he says, and adds the final promise that the heavenly Father will "give the Holy Spirit to those who ask him" (Luke 11:9-13). St. Paul's prayer at the close of Ephesians 3 is just that kind of asking:

*For this reason I bow my knees before the Father, from whom every family in heaven and on earth is named, that according to the riches of his glory he may grant you to be strengthened with might through his Spirit in the inner man, and that Christ may dwell in your hearts through faith; that you, being rooted and grounded in love may have power to comprehend with all the saints what is the breadth and length and height and depth, and to know the love of Christ which surpasses knowledge, that you may be filled with all the fulness of God.*

The Lord sees his church in the midst of Enochville, and loves it. He pours out his Spirit with renewed gifts of understanding and love, freedom and boldness. As hearts are filled, tongues are also loosed. The water of life, once drunk, flows out like a river (John 7:38). Let Enochville become "wise," therefore, and "serve the Lord with fear, and rejoice with trembling" (Psalm 2:10-11 AV). For the church, founded on a rock, is attacking Cain's walls. And his gates shall not prevail against it (Matthew 16:18).

The Lord has neither sold out to Cain, nor given up on him. He wants him home.

## Epilogue

# *THE VIEW FROM THE MOUNTAIN*

*And in the Spirit he carried me away to a great, high mountain, and showed me the holy city Jerusalem coming down out of heaven from God, having the glory of God.* Revelation 21:10-11

Will it ever happen that the walls of Enochville fall, and that Cain comes home?

Isaiah had visions of such a day. "The Spirit of the Lord" would rest on a "branch" from Jesse's roots, "the spirit of wisdom and understanding, the spirit of counsel and might, the spirit of knowledge and the fear of the Lord." He would judge "with righteousness," and "smite the earth with the rod of his mouth," that is, with the true weapon of the Word of God. In that day, "The wolf shall dwell with the lamb . . . They shall not hurt or destroy in all my holy mountain; for the earth shall be full of the knowledge of the Lord as the waters cover the sea." (Isaiah 11:1-9)

By all the realism of human experience, it is an impossible dream. The strong still devour the weak, as the wolf does the lamb. The Lord remains unknown in Enochville, and to a tragic degree even in his church. Jesus, within his own people, found himself up against ears that would not hear and hearts that would not understand (Matthew 13:15; Isaiah 6:10). "When the Son of man comes," he cried, "will he find faith on earth?" (Luke 18:8) And yet the kingdom came. In the world's great darkness he shone as the one true light. By his death the darkness was overcome and the curse broken. Righteousness and the knowledge of God triumphed. A lost world, all unknowing, gained a reprieve full of life and of hope.

Those who have been drawn to the light see and know the glory of God in the face of Christ. They share both his death and his resurrection. Death has no power over them, for Jesus has prepared for them a room in his Father's house (John 14:1-2). On the day of God's final intervention and judgment, the earth as we know it will perish together with all the proud works in which Enochville glories. The saints will then inherit the new heavens and the new earth in which righteousness dwells (Matthew 13:41-43; 1 Thessalonians 4:13-5:11; 2 Peter 3:8-13). Exactly what such futurist language implies we cannot know now. It will be revealed in its time, with a glory and truth beyond anything our imagination can foresee or our words utter. But the promises stand sure, and for the saints who know God that is enough.

Other texts envision the future in terms not so much of a sudden cataclysmic event, as of a slow process already begun. A man scatters seed; it sprouts and grows, "he knows not how" (Mark 4:26-29). The kingdom is like "the smallest of all seeds" which grows incomprehensibly and unnoticed until it has become "the greatest of shrubs . . . a tree, so that the birds of the air come and make nests in its branches" (Matthew 13:31-32). A woman hides a bit of leaven in three measures of meal and, by a process beyond her thought, the whole is eventually leavened (Matthew 13:33).

St. Paul seems to take the large view of such a process as he marvels over the depth of God's wisdom and knowledge. Long ago, Yahweh in his strange will and mercy chose an enslaved people, Israel, to be his own, quite disregarding the glory of Pharaoh and the nations. Now, it appears, Israel's opposition to the word of the cross has opened the way for these nations, formerly excluded, to be grafted into the root of God's people. But ahead lies the day when Israel is provoked to "jealousy" and is thereby restored fully to the heritage God had always intended for his beloved. Thus "all Israel," Jew and Gentile alike, the brothers Abel and Cain alike, the whole of humanity, "will be saved" (Romans 9-11). All humanity, full of the knowledge of the Lord! That is God's grand design! And this vision carries the Apostle on, filled with hope and energy in the Spirit, to preach the Gospel of Christ without embarrassment or fear "from Jerusalem and as far round as Illyricum" (Romans 15:19).

The gift of the Holy Spirit includes the capacity of the people of God to "see visions" and to "dream dreams" (Acts 2:17; Joel 2:28). The Lord lifts their eyes high above the oppressing burdens and the impossible tasks and the helpless frustrations so obvious to the natural sight. He took Moses high up on Mount Nebo, so that he could see far and thus grasp in one sweep the land promised to Israel (Deuteronomy 34:1-4). He sent Abraham on a grand tour of the land his descendants would possess (Genesis 13:14-17). It was no accident that the devil took Jesus "to a very high mountain, and showed him all the kingdoms of the world and the glory of them" (Matthew 4:8), for the force of the temptation was to mimic and thus mock the promises of God. The Gospel of Matthew closes with the scene on the mountain in Galilee, where the risen Jesus sets the vision of "all nations" before the disciples and sends them on the mission of universal conquest—not by the sword, but by the foolishness of preaching, teaching, and baptizing in the name of the Father, Son, and Holy Spirit (Matthew 28:16-20).

The closing chapters of the Bible also invite us to stand on a mountain of vision, with John of Patmos (Revelation 21-22). Not from Enochville, but from heaven there comes the bride of the Lamb, the holy city Jerusalem, founded on Calvary, God's new creation. The heaven and earth which Cain knew in his alienation has passed away. The sea, source of all the sin and oppression humanity has ever experienced, is no more. A great voice from the throne of God explains what it all means. "The dwelling of God is with men." God is not far off, hidden, his face turned away. He has made his home within humanity. No more tears, therefore, or death, or mourning, or pain! The former things, all the forces of Enochville's alienation, have passed away. Here now is God's holy city, publicly displayed, magnificent in its jeweled splendor, clean, transparent, clear as crystal! Away with Enochville's proud architecture and artistry! No man shall design or build the temple of this Jerusalem. God is himself its temple and its light. All nations rejoice to have part in it, to pour their wealth and their glory into it.

The city is also wide open—no gates, no walls, no dangerous night. No need for locks and defenses. No fear! No one is shut out. Even Cain the murderer has free access, for all who enter share one common treasure—the Lamb who redeemed them to God by his blood (Revelation 5:9). The "unclean" and those who "practice abomination or falsehood" are not to be found in it, not because the city is closed to them, but because they still prefer their old wisdom of knowing good and evil to the truth and glory of God. To such the city of God remains invisible. They "cannot see it." The crystal transparency of its purity and truth is too much for them. They want only what they can see, handle, and control. They want only Enochville.

The life of God himself fills the holy city. Out of God's throne and the Lamb's, there flows a river of pure water, the Word of God, right through the middle of everything. The water creates life wherever it touches. The tree of life grows on its banks, bearing abundant fruit for every month of the year, offering its leaves for the healing of the nations. Here the saints live and serve their God. His name is on their foreheads, identifying them as his own. They are free of fear and of darkness. They reign with the Lamb for ever and ever.

That is the vision. Suddenly we grasp more fully what we are seeing. At first it appeared to be a vision of the future. By the time it has unfolded to the end, however, we realize that God is showing us the city that is already here, right now, in the midst of Enochville. It embraces in its radiant citizenship all who confess Jesus and find wisdom and hope in his promises. These are the saints who serve God day and night even now (Revelation 7:15). They drink the living water and eat the fruit of the tree of life. They are not afraid. The darkness of Enochville cannot dismay or hurt them. They only long for Cain to see their city and its glory, to enter and be cleansed and free, to meet and know God again.

It is good to ascend the mountain of vision, and to return to it again and again in moments of testing and of deep discouragement.

But we do not remain on the mountain. We turn our eyes willingly back to Enochville. For Enochville in its own way is God's city, too, bearing the mark of Cain and upheld by a hidden mercy of God even through his judgments. To descend from the mountain is to enter Enochville fully, to belong there by God's own will, to participate in its trials, to risk and endure its anger, pride, despair, division, frustration, and futility. That is the front line of Yahweh's battle. That is where God wants his people to be. To infect Cain's city with the leaven of Christ is simply their calling. There is a life to be lived, a work to be done.

> *The Spirit and the Bride say, "Come." And let him who hears say "Come." And let him who is thirsty come, let him who desires take the water of life without price.* (Revelation 22: 17)

Cain! Come home!

# *APPENDIX*

This book is written for Christians in churches, and not particularly for scholars. Like a sermon, it draws on a text and carries a theme through to its final consequences. For this reason I have offered no footnotes, other than the biblical references within the text.

I would, however, also welcome its examination by people who are especially trained in biblical studies. Toward that possibility, I would call to attention three exegetical findings of my own which pervade the book and are fundamental to its argument. They need to be put to the test by others.

1. I take the designation "my beloved Son" at Jesus' baptism (Matthew 3:17) to derive from Exodus 4:22-23, "Israel is my first-born son." My argument for this finding appears in *Journal of Biblical Literature,* LXXXVII (1968), 301-311, under the title, "Exodus 4:22-23 and the Voice from Heaven." The thesis, that the name "Son of God" has as its first significance Jesus' identification in and with Israel, is fundamental to my reconstruction of his temptations and ministry, and of the climax of his passion (see especially chapters 4 and 5).

2. The concept of "the knowledge of good and evil," which I develop in the first chapter and then use throughout the book, is also my own finding. I came close to it in my study of Jesus' temptations (doctoral dissertation at Concordia Seminary, St. Louis, 1966). The real break-through came in the fall of 1966, however, when I was conducting a pro-seminar on temptation and the fall at Valparaiso

University. It was triggered by Dietrich Bonhoeffer who, in his *Creation and Fall,* explains "knowing good and evil" in terms of "distinguishing between pleasure and pain." A little later, in exploring the consequences of the fall, Bonhoeffer associates pleasure and pain with the emotions of "passion and hate." Though Bonhoeffer's treatment on the whole pursues a different track than mine, these became the categories which brought unity to all my previous study of temptation and sin, and which opened new directions of associated ideas I had never dreamed of. I developed this theme in print for the first time in *The Holy Infection* (St. Louis: Concordia Publishing House, 1969, pp. 21ff. and throughout). Though I have found it in no commentator, Christian or Jewish, it has become for me a precious key toward understanding the biblical diagnosis of sin, as well as the battle of Christ and the transforming power and victory of the Gospel. Without it, this book would not exist.

3. A third finding has to do with my interpretation, in the first chapter, of Genesis 4:4-5, "The Lord had regard for Abel and his offering, but for Cain and his offering he had no regard" (RSV). This interpretation, too, is fundamental to this book. It is necessary to explore it further, since it seems to conflict with what might appear to be an alternative (and in the view of some, the authoritative) interpretation in Hebrews 11:4. Since nothing of my view has appeared in print previously, a more extensive examination of this question is offered here.

The Hebrew word translated "have regard for" (AV, "have respect") is *sha'ah.* Its basic meaning is simply "look." The verb is quite rare. In all the Old Testament it occurs only fifteen times, and then in such a variety of usage as to call for many different renderings. None of the other occurrences is sufficiently parallel to our text to be helpful. I would prefer to translate more neutrally than is usually done, however, so as to avoid suggesting a divine attitude of approval or disapproval: "The Lord paid attention to Abel and his offering, but to Cain and his offering he paid no attention."

Though the verb *sha'ah* is rare, the idea that God looks upon his people, or does not look upon them, is very common and is expressed by a variety of terms. Instances in which God is described as looking in order to see and judge sin (e.g., Genesis 6:5, 12; 18:21) do not really parallel our text, and we shall pass them by here.

Of immediate concern are references in which his "looking" implies his favor and help, so that the person looked upon experiences blessing. A prayer for God to "look" constitutes an appeal for deliverance from some affliction. A man upon whom the Lord does not "look" is a man afflicted.

For example, if the Lord will only *see* (*ra'ah*) the one afflicted, deliverance is sure to come (Genesis 29:31-35; 2 Samuel 16:12; Psalm 25:18; 80:14). When he *visits* or *cares for* (*paqad*) the earth or his people, his goodness is concretely experienced (Psalm 8:4; 65:9; 80:14; cf. Luke 1:68; 7:16). Divine blessing is implied also in passages which state that God is *mindful of* (*zakar,* Psalm 8:4), *turns to* or *regards* (*panah,* Psalm 102:17; 119:132), *makes his face shine* (*or,* Numbers 6:25; Psalm 67:1; 80:19; 119:135), *looks down* (*nabat,* Psalm 80:14; 84:9), or has *his eye on* his people (Psalm 33:18).

On the other hand, the experience of distress is implied when the Lord *sleeps, forgets,* and *hides his face* (Psalm 44:23-24; 22:24; 30:7), or when he *forsakes* (Psalm 22:1; 71:11) or is *far away* (Psalm 71:12) or *despises* (Psalm 22:24; 51:17; 102:17), or when he does not look, see, visit, and cause his face to shine (Psalm 80:14). Human experience is thus expressed in the language of God's apparent attitude. This association of experience with attitude may be illustrated from 1 Samuel 10:27. In connection with Saul's assumption of the kingship, we are told that "Some worthless fellows . . . *despised* him and *brought him no present.*" The failure to bring a gift makes the despising visible. In fact, the two terms mean the same thing.

A few additional examples may help us become more sensitive to this use of language. God's intervention in Egypt, according to the narrative of the exodus, began with his remembering and paying attention to the children of Israel. "God *heard* their groaning, and God *remembered* his covenant with Abraham, with Isaac, and with Jacob. And God *knew* their condition." (Exodus 2:24-25; similarly 3:7; 4:31; Deuteronomy 26:7-8) The language implies that in Israel's long bondage up to that crucial turning point, God had *not* been hearing, remembering, seeing, and knowing them. We can understand the vivid force of such language. The question we face as interpreters, however, is whether we have the right to absolutize such expressions as though they were able or even intended to encompass the whole of what God is and is doing in relation to his people.

That question becomes vivid in Psalm 44, a prayer spoken out of grave affliction. It is by no means a penitential prayer. This Psalmist is not confessing sins. On the contrary, he finds the experience of disaster which God has now laid on his people simply inexplicable. "All this has come upon us, though we have not forgotten thee, or been false to thy covenant" (Psalm 44:17). Then comes the climactic plea, "*Rouse thyself!* Why *sleepest* thou, O Lord? *Awake!* Do not cast us off forever! Why dost thou *hide thy face*? Why dost thou *forget* our affliction and oppression? . . . *Rise up, come* to our help! Deliver us for the sake of thy steadfast love!" (verses 23-26). The experience of distress and affliction testifies that God is sleeping, hiding, forgetting. But a hidden question remains, and we may be sure the Psalmist is aware of it. Does the knowledge of God's attitude which derives from our experience of prosperity or adversity exhaust the truth of God? Is there not another way of knowing God—one which defies experience, and depends solely on God's unfailing word and promise?

Similarly Psalm 80:14, "*Turn* again, O God of hosts'. *Look down* from heaven, and *see; have regard for* this vine, the stock which thy right hand planted." Also verse 19, "Restore us, O Lord God of hosts! Let *thy face shine,* that we may be saved." If only God will *look at* his people, they will be delivered. The look and the deliverance are of a piece.

The paradox with which Habakkuk wrestles in 1:13 is most dramatic. In the face of the impending Babylonian invasion, looming in all terror so quickly after the fall of Assyria, the prophet cries out to God, "Thou who art of purer *eyes* than to *behold* evil and canst not *look on* wrong, why dost thou *look on* faithless men, and art *silent* when the wicked swallows up the man more righteous than he?" God is "looking on" the pagan invader. The language means that God is granting him blessing and success, even against God's own people! Toward Israel, on the other hand, God is blind, deaf, and dumb! The prophet does not ask *whether* that is so, but *why*. Yet even in his anguish, he knows that what men see and interpret out of their experience does not exhaust the knowledge of

God. Therefore, he pleads that the "vision" is not complete, but "awaits its time," and he summons Israel to hang on in faith to the word and promises of God, even against sight (Habakkuk 2:2-4). His book concludes with a magnificent confession of such faith, a stirring refusal to read God's mind and attitude out of mere human experience:

> *Though the fig tree do not blossom,*
> *nor fruit be on the vines,*
> *the produce of the olive fail*
> *and the fields yield no food,*
> *the flock be cut off from the fold*
> *and there be no herd in the stalls,*
> *yet will I rejoice in the Lord,*
> *I will joy in the God of my salvation.*
> (Habakkuk 3:17-18)

This is the quiet and stubborn beauty of a living faith. It calls sight the liar, and chooses to rest not in the logic of human inference, but in the word and arms of the living God.

A parallel drama of faith against sight unfolds in Psalm 22, whose first verse Jesus takes up as his own cry on the cross, "My God, my God, why hast thou forsaken me." As in Habakkuk and in Psalm 44, the question is not "whether" but "why". For there is no evidence of God, no sound from or sight of him. The total disaster, as experienced by the Psalmist and by Jesus, testifies to nothing but abandonment. Faith and obedience appear to have been altogether in vain. Victory has gone to the enemy. And yet the cry of dereliction is not the last word! In the whole Psalm, faith goes to war against sight, faith in God for what he has done and has promised, and will still do. By faith the Psalmist emerges triumphant, as does Jesus.

This is the context of thought and language in which Genesis 4: 4-5 needs to be read, "The Lord paid attention to Abel and his offering, but to Cain and his offering he paid no attention." The language is that of sight and inference, and expresses the contrasting experiences of prosperity and of adversity, that is, of "good" over against "evil." But it only raises, and does not yet answer, the fundamental question. For the knowledge of Yahweh is not exhausted when someone finds occasion to exclaim, "Somebody up there likes me!" or its converse, "Somebody up there has it in for me!" As St. Paul reminds us in Romans 11:34, "Who has known the mind of the Lord?"

Thus the story of Cain and Abel, like that of Eve (Genesis 3: 1-6), is a temptation story in which the word of God and faith is opposed to sight and inference. By sight Cain infers that Yahweh is not being fair to him. But could he not give up on sight and inference so as to trust God, even in the face of what looks like rebuke and disapproval? Could he not by faith cast himself on the mercy of the very God who seems to be hurting him? Could he not let the "vision" await its time (Habakkuk 2:3-4), so as to see what strange outcome Yahweh's own mysterious "knowledge of good and evil" may intend? This is what Yahweh is pleading for when he summons Cain to master the sin which is couching at the door.

Apparently no commentator has understood the temptation of Cain in this way, however. Interpreters have generally assumed, just as Cain did, that Yahweh's looking or not looking expresses a response to something he likes about Abel or does not like in Cain. Therefore, the task of interpretation has been to discover the variable in the brothers so as to account for Yahweh's varied reaction. The highly speculative outcome may be illustrated from Flavius Josephus, a first century Jewish (Pharisaic) historian. Abel, according to Josephus, was "a lover of righteousness" who "excelled in virtue." Cain was "wicked," "wholly intent on getting" (here Josephus plays on the meaning of Cain's name). Abel's offering of "milk and the first-fruits of his flocks" honored God, for these "grew naturally" of their own accord. Cain's offering "was the invention of a covetous man, and gotten by forcing the ground." This explains why "God was more delighted" with Abel's offering than with Cain's. Josephus does not seem to notice that the Lord God had manifested no such antipathy toward agriculture in Genesis 2:15 (*Antiquities* II, 1, William Whiston's translation).

Notice, however, what kind of lesson such an interpretation would impress on the pious reader. God's people, if they wish to be accepted and to please God, must take care to reproduce in themselves and in their sacrificial works the quality of righteousness represented in Abel. They must avoid being like Cain. Thus the hearer is driven to become the more self-conscious and introspective regarding his works and inner piety. He is made to anticipate a verdict, and becomes either satisfied or fearful, depending on what he is able to see in himself and on the outcome he anticipates for his efforts. A narrative whose original intent was to call for faith in the prior mercy, wisdom, and unfailing promises of Yahweh, has thereby been made to teach the righteousness of man's inner piety and external works.

This book, therefore, proceeds on the understanding, confirmed by many texts, that the difference in Yahweh's treatment of the brothers does not stand in any relationship of cause and effect deriving from differences in Cain and Abel. Rather, it expresses Yahweh's freedom in his own mercy and wisdom to deal with people "unequally." The issue is universal, and very human. It confronts Cain (and Abel) with the root temptation which leads to Cain's fall and alienation.

There is a further complication, however, which needs to be shared. My interpretation differs not only from that of traditional commentaries, but also (apparently, at least) from an interpretation assumed within the New Testament Scriptures, specifically at 1 John 3:11-12 and Hebrews 11:4.

I have dealt with the first of these texts in the fourth chapter. Cain is presented as having murdered his brother "because his own deeds were evil and his brother's righteous." A close examination of parallel texts in the Gospel of John (John 3:19-20; 8:39-44; 8:45-47; 15:18-25) suggests strongly that the apostle is in reality using the original Cain and Abel story as a kind of parable for the death of Jesus at the hand of his "brother," namely the Jews. It is precarious, therefore, to read John's mind as though we could determine by way of this text just how he would interpret Genesis 4 if that were his direct intention.

Hebrews 11:4 presents a similar difficulty: "By faith Abel offered to God a more acceptable sacrifice than Cain, through which he received approval as righteous, God bearing witness by accepting his gifts; he died, but through his faith he is still speaking."

Here the holy writer seems clearly to assume the kind of interpretation I have rejected. God's regarding or not regarding signifies a divine verdict, which distinguishes between the brothers on the basis of some quality God sees in them and in their sacrifices. The initial phrase, "By faith," introduces a distinctively New Testament insight, however. In its background lies the notion that Abel's offering proceeded from what St. Paul calls "the righteousness of faith" over against the "righteousness of the law" which characterized Cain's (Romans 10:1-6). Hence this text too, like that of 1 John 3, is colored by insights which derive from the passing of the Old Testament into the New through Jesus' death and resurrection. The writer's purpose in Hebrews 11 is to show, by illustrations out of Old Testament and pre-Christian history, that "faith" has always been the motivating power for the obedience of God's people and for their willingness to suffer. It is as a martyr, corresponding to Christian experiences of martyrdom, that Abel "through his faith is still speaking."

If we view Hebrews 11:4 in the context of its purpose, we encounter no great difficulty. But if we go beyond and seek to impose Hebrews 11:4 as the Holy Spirit's own authoritative interpretation of Genesis 4 (thus prohibiting any further searching of what the story may have intended in its original writing), we encounter all kinds of difficulty.

What is this "faith" then, which Abel had and Cain lacked? By definition, faith must have a word of promise to which it can cling (Romans 10:14-17). What then is the "word" to which Abel clung by faith as he brought his sacrifice, and which Cain despised? This is not at all clear, not even in Hebrews 11:4. Indeed, the simple reader, if he presses the question, is only too likely to forget that faith must have a promise. He is likely to imagine rather that Abel's "faith" is an internal quality like "sincerity," and that Cain's offering was merely an external performance lacking such sincerity. It follows that the reader, if he is at all serious about this text as God's word, must begin to examine his own sacrificing and works, to see whether he has been garnishing them with a sufficient measure of "sincerity" to please God. But now his very effort to be "faith-ful" has the debilitating effect of making him "faith-less." For his eye is no longer turned to the word of God, to baptism and the cross in which God has spoken to him the word of forgiveness and of life without any conditions. His eye is turned rather on himself! He has been driven into the very self-consciousness regarding his own performance which St. Paul opposes as deadly (Romans 9:30-10:4)! Ignorant of the righteousness that comes from God, he is seeking to establish a righteousness of his own, all in the name of a false conception of "faith."

The Holy Spirit of Christ does not contradict himself that way. To force him to do so, as though for the sake of upholding the authority of Scripture to interpret Scripture, by superficially wresting a text out of its context and imposing it where it does not belong, actually subverts the Holy Scriptures, however reverent and "faithful" the motive may be.

Hebrews 11:4 must be left in the New Testament, where it is. If anyone presses the question further, why the writer of Hebrews understood and used the Cain story as he did, let him speculate as he will. I hold only that Genesis 4 is the clear text, and that Hebrews 11:4, if brought into association with it, is unclear. The unclear must always be interpreted by the clear, and above all by the clarity of the Gospel of Jesus Christ our Lord.

# INDEX OF BIBLICAL CITATIONS